Coloring Book for Adult and Kids
Beautiful Horse Pattern

By
Nisita Noojui

Benefits of Adult Coloring Books?

Coloring books are not just for the kids anymore. In fact, adult coloring books are all the rage right now. It is a fun activity for many children and adults. It has been shown to have stress and anxiety reducing benefits. Coloring books can make you feel calmer, mentally clearer, happier, and more relaxed. Also, it helps you focus and creativity. Although coloring is not an incredibly demanding activity, it still needs your focus and attention while engaged with a picture.

How to Color!
You can use markers, colored pencils, gel pens, or pens for coloring

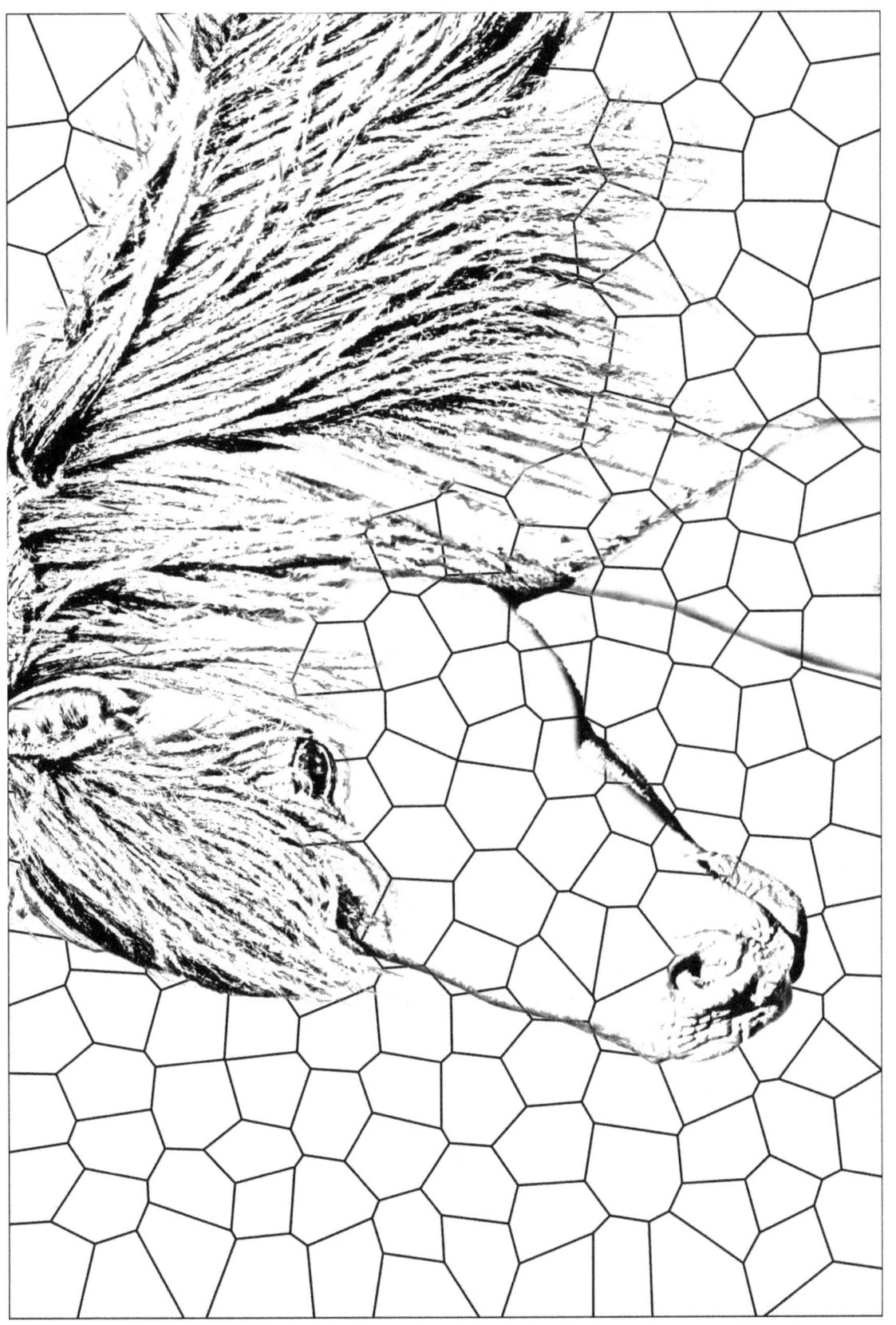

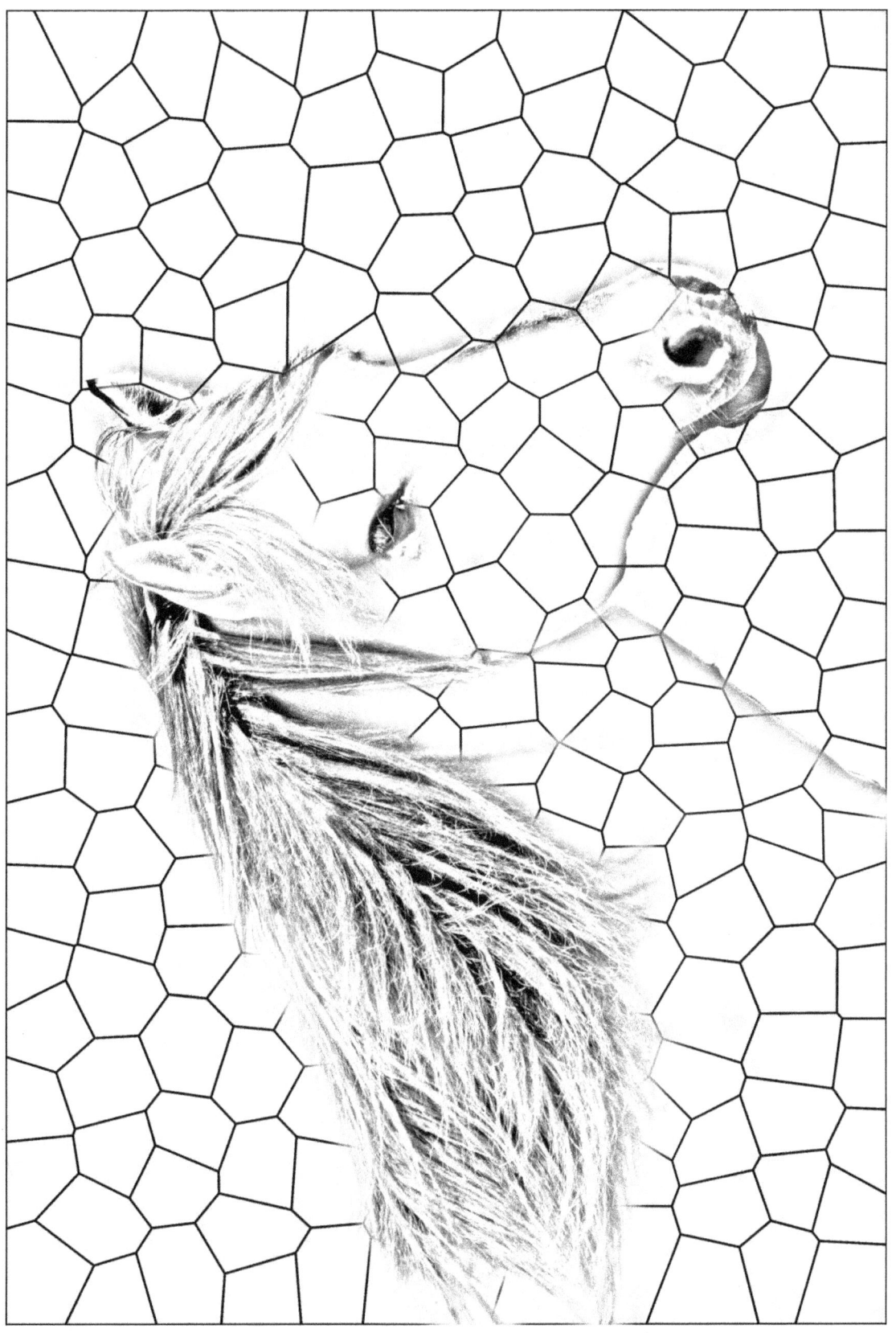

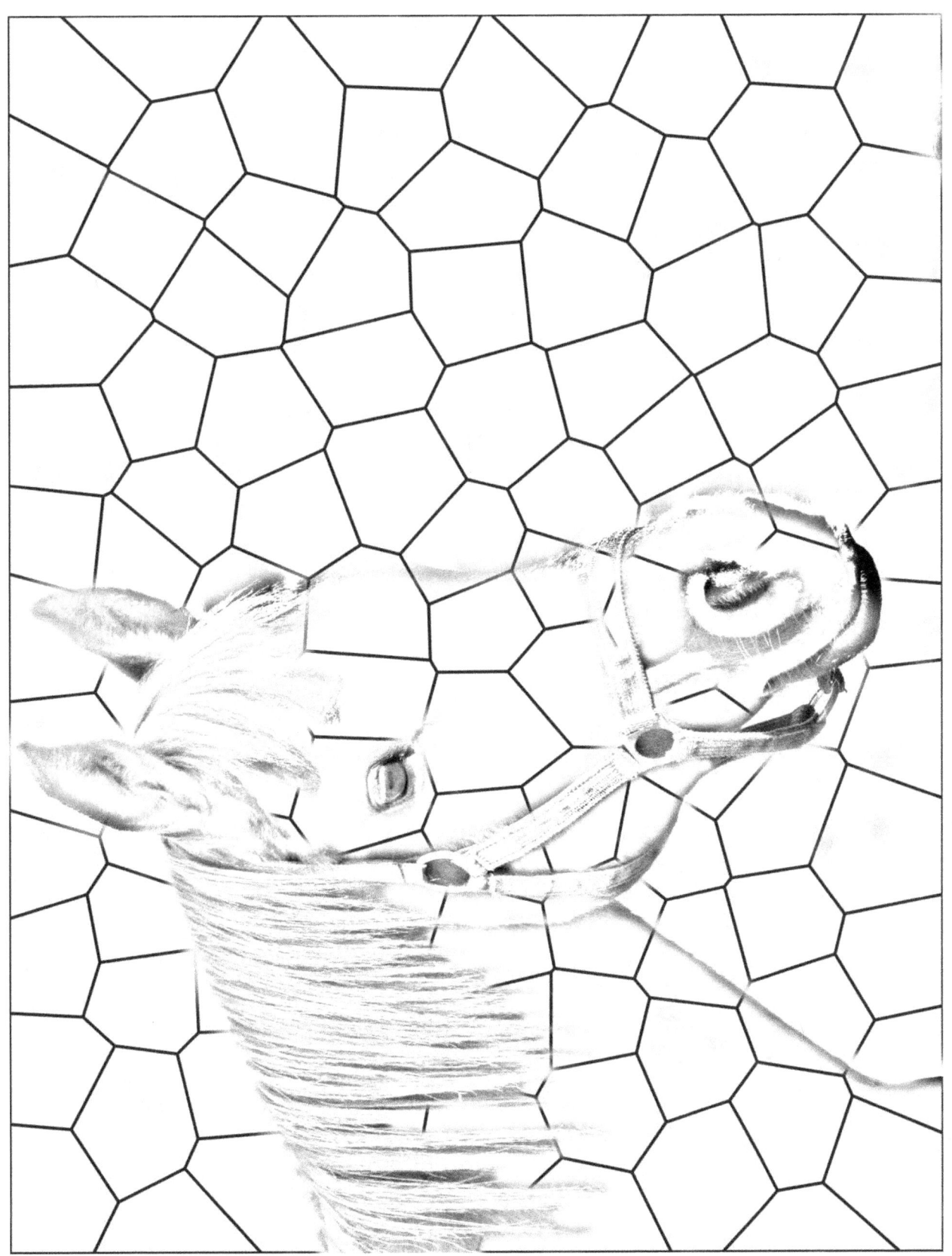

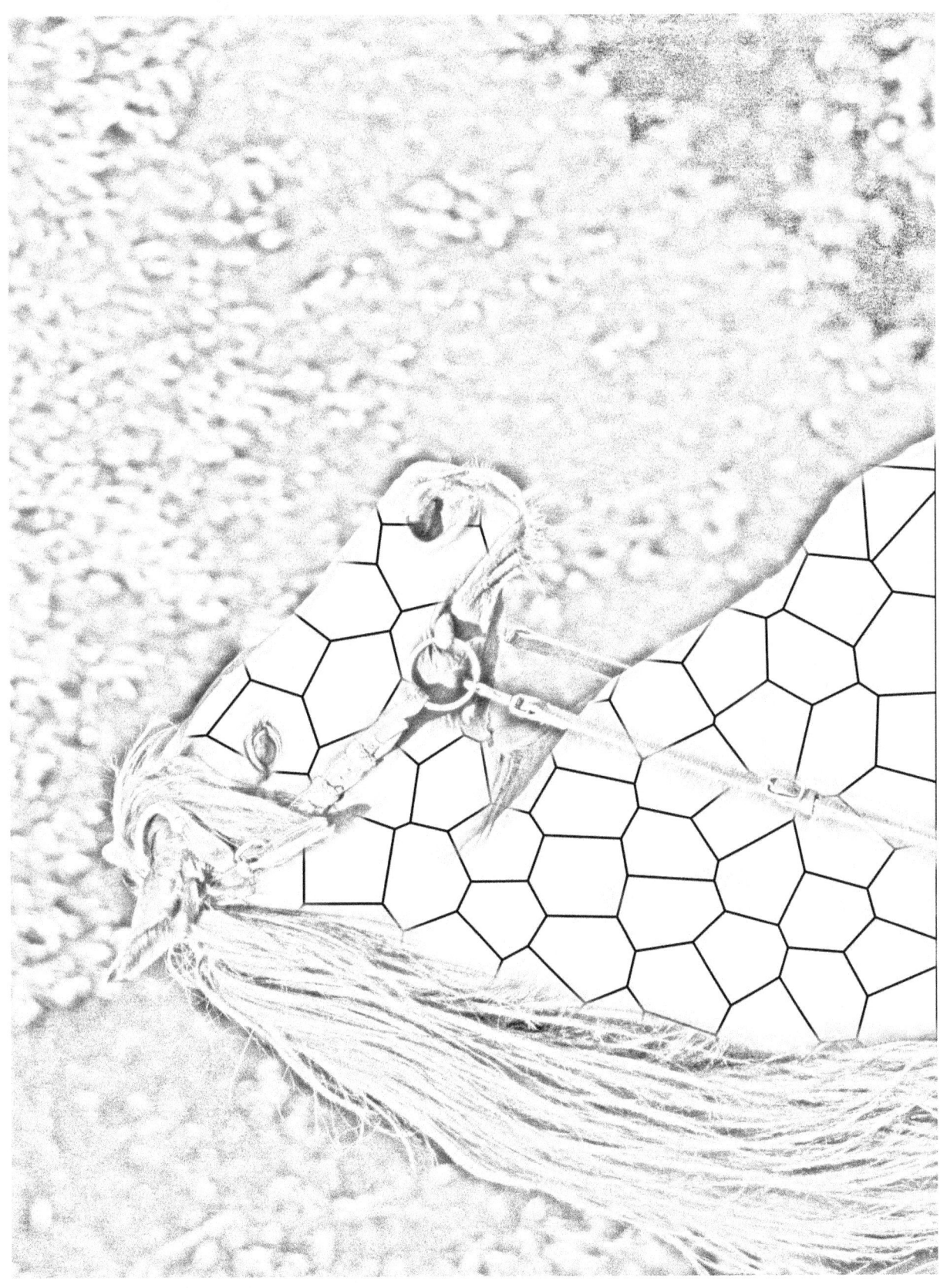

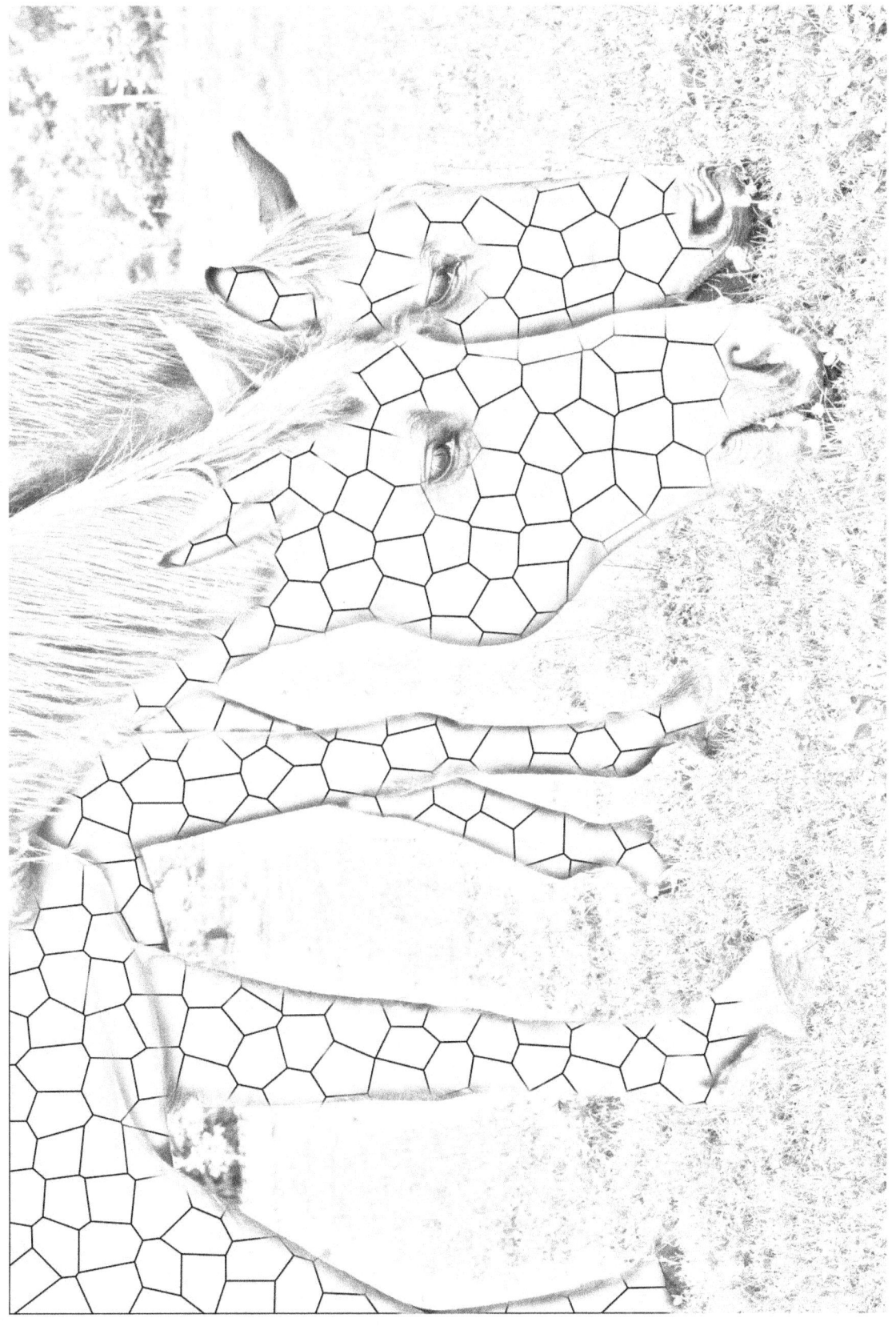

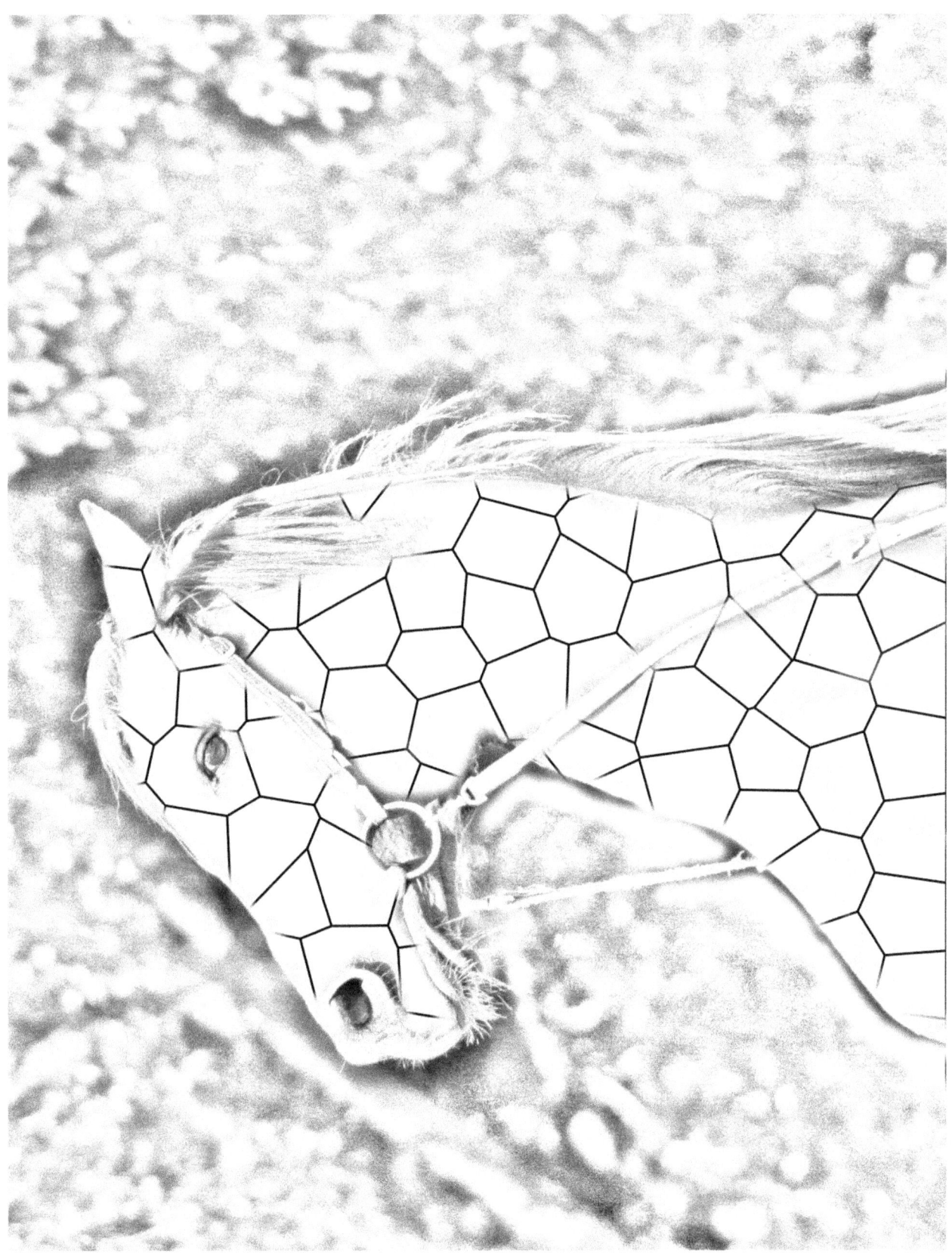

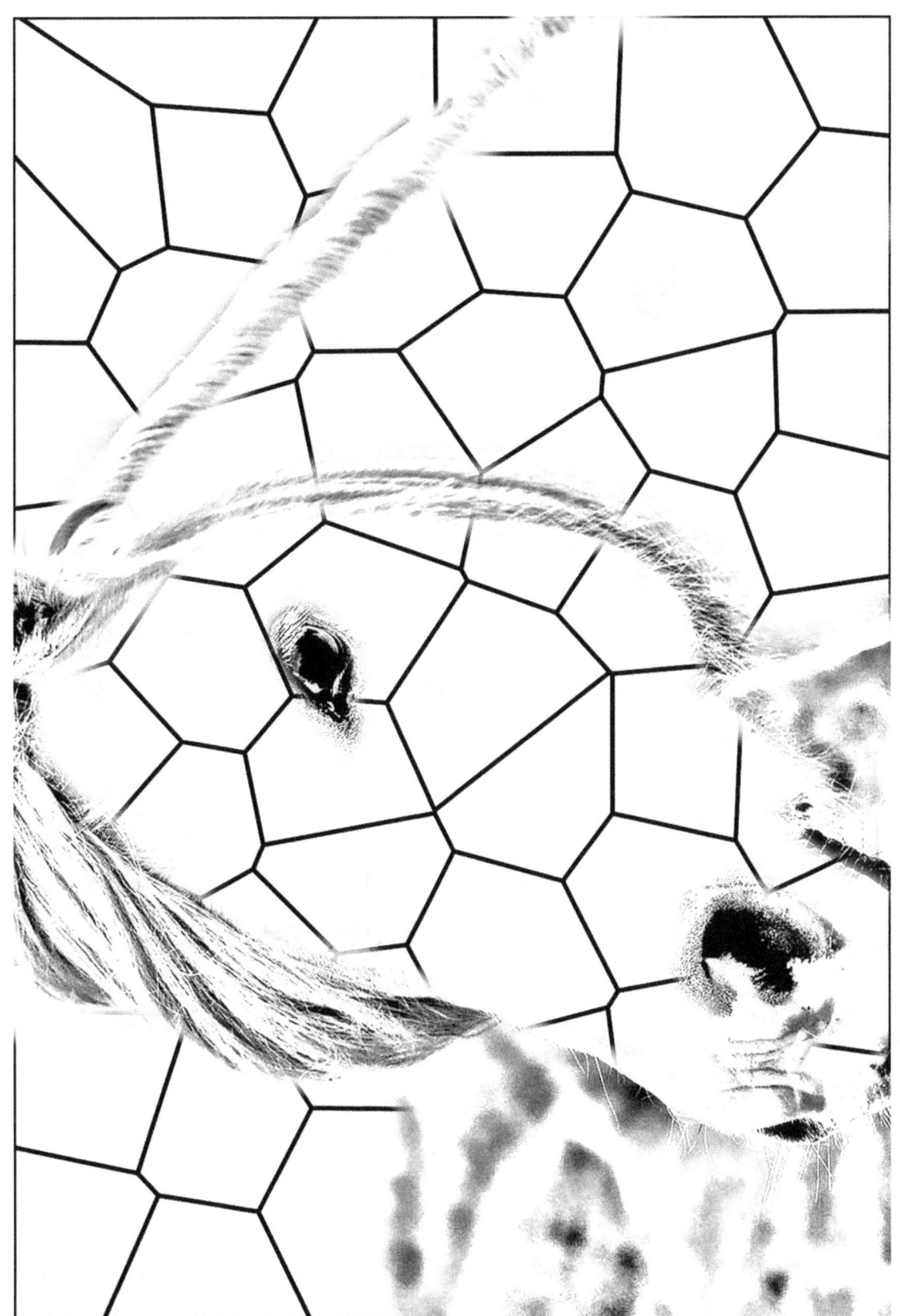

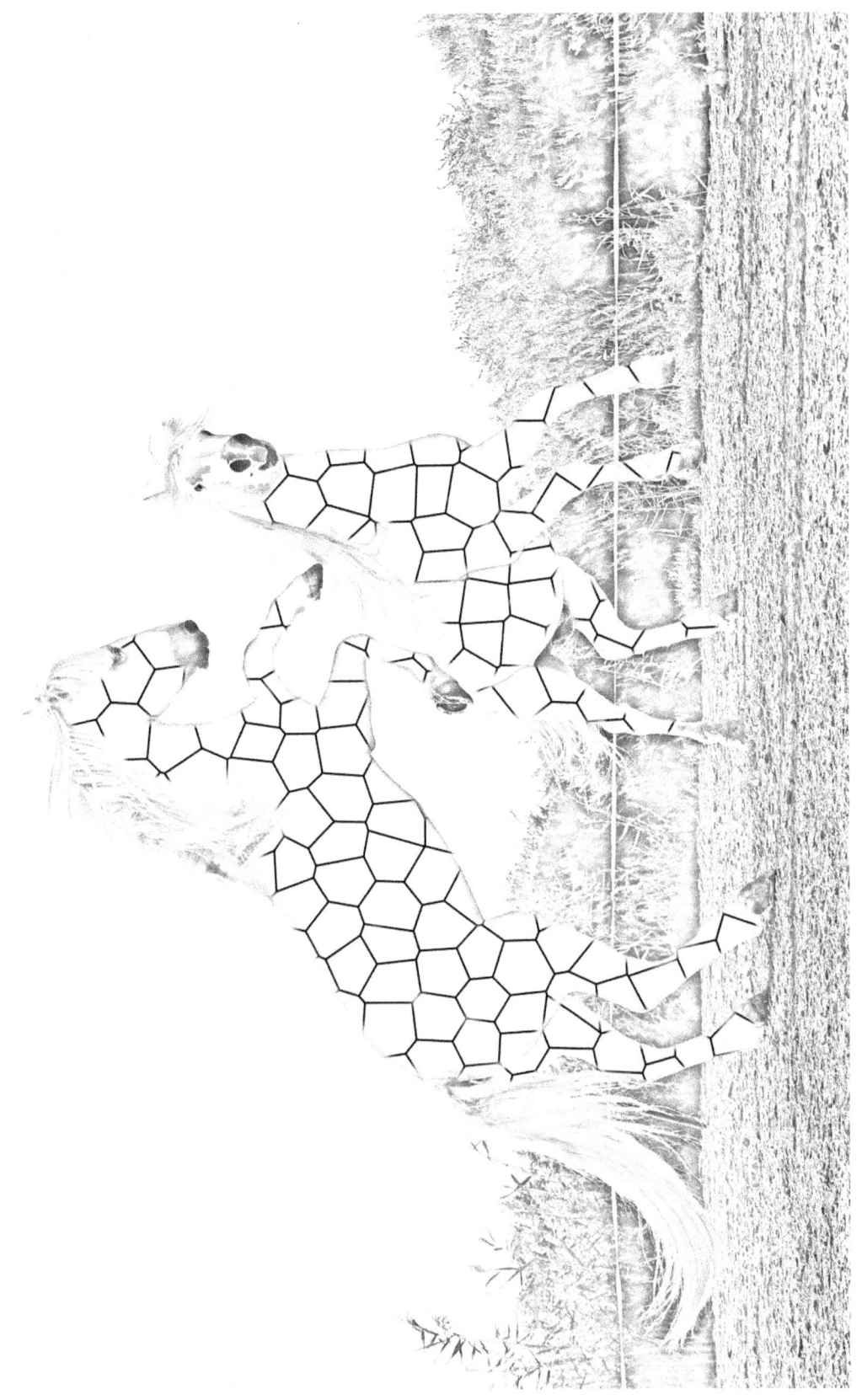

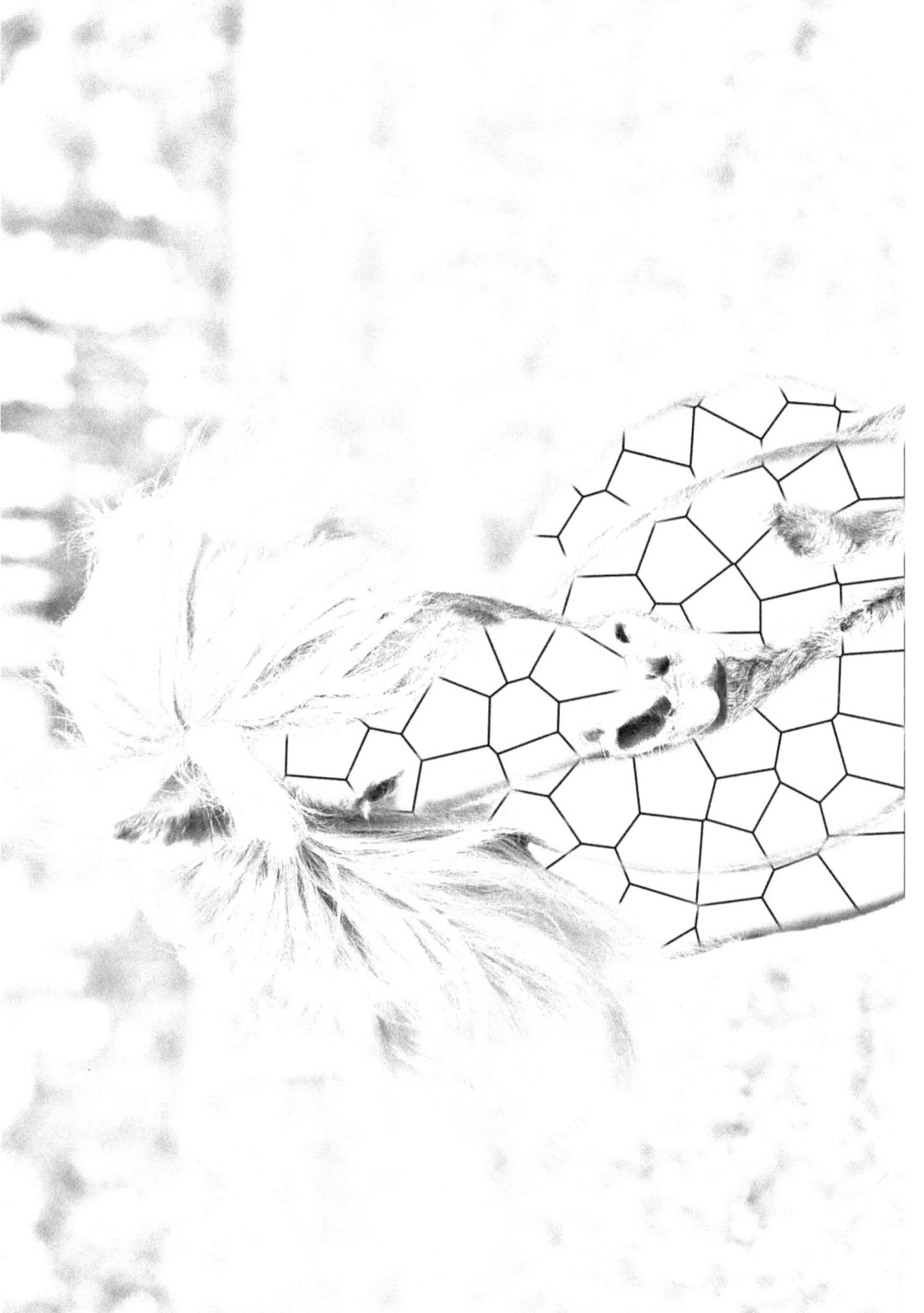

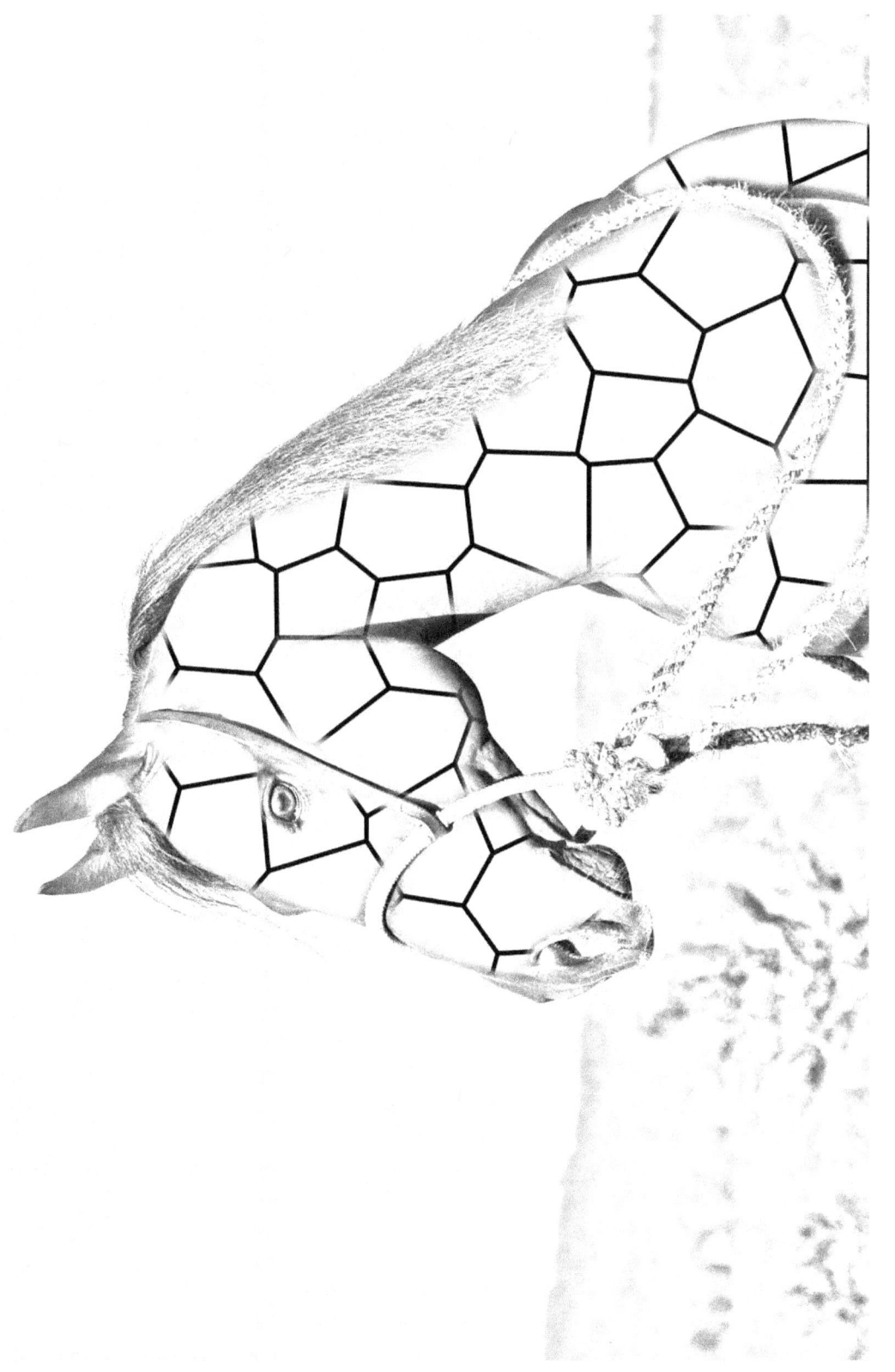

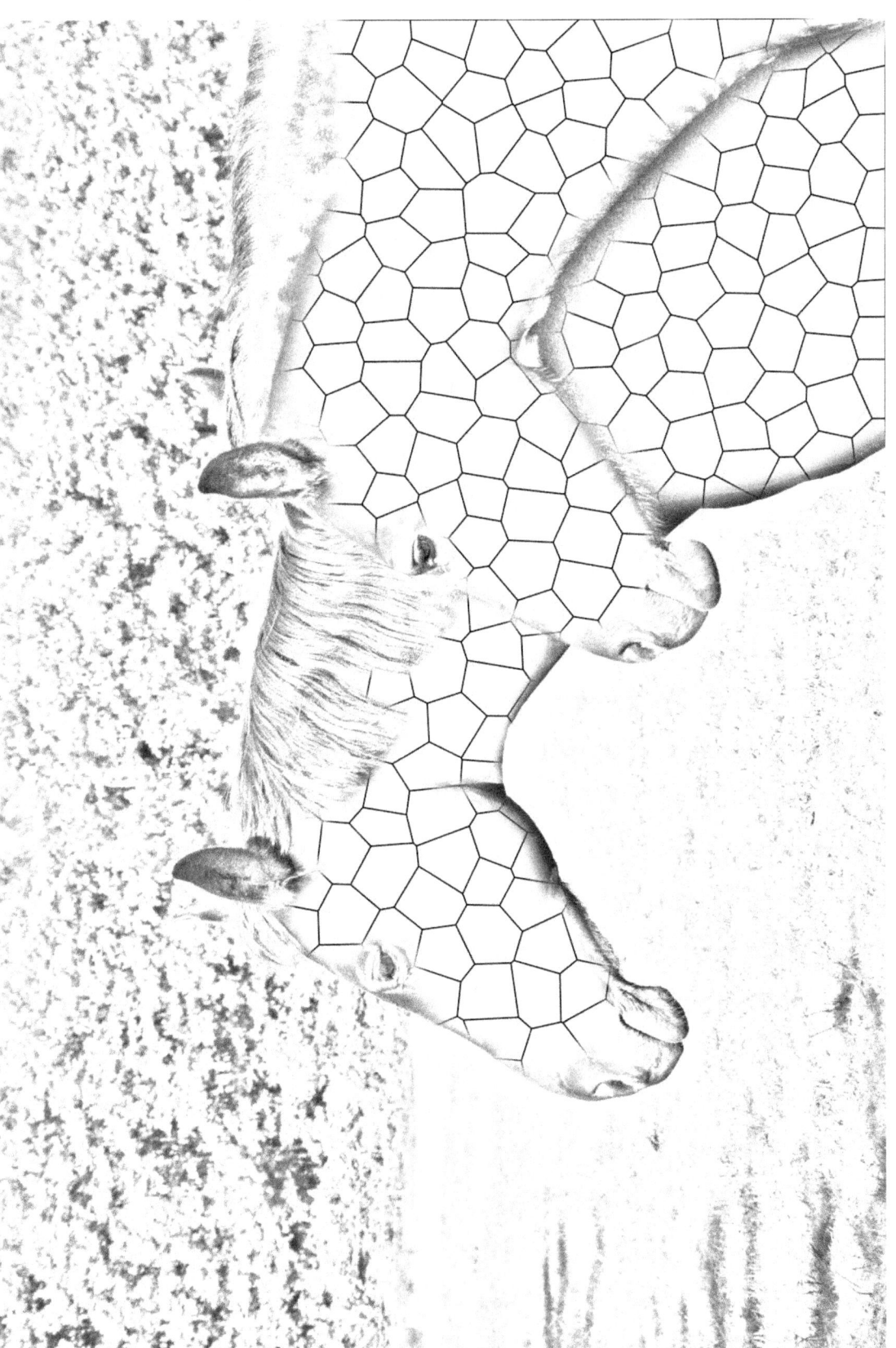

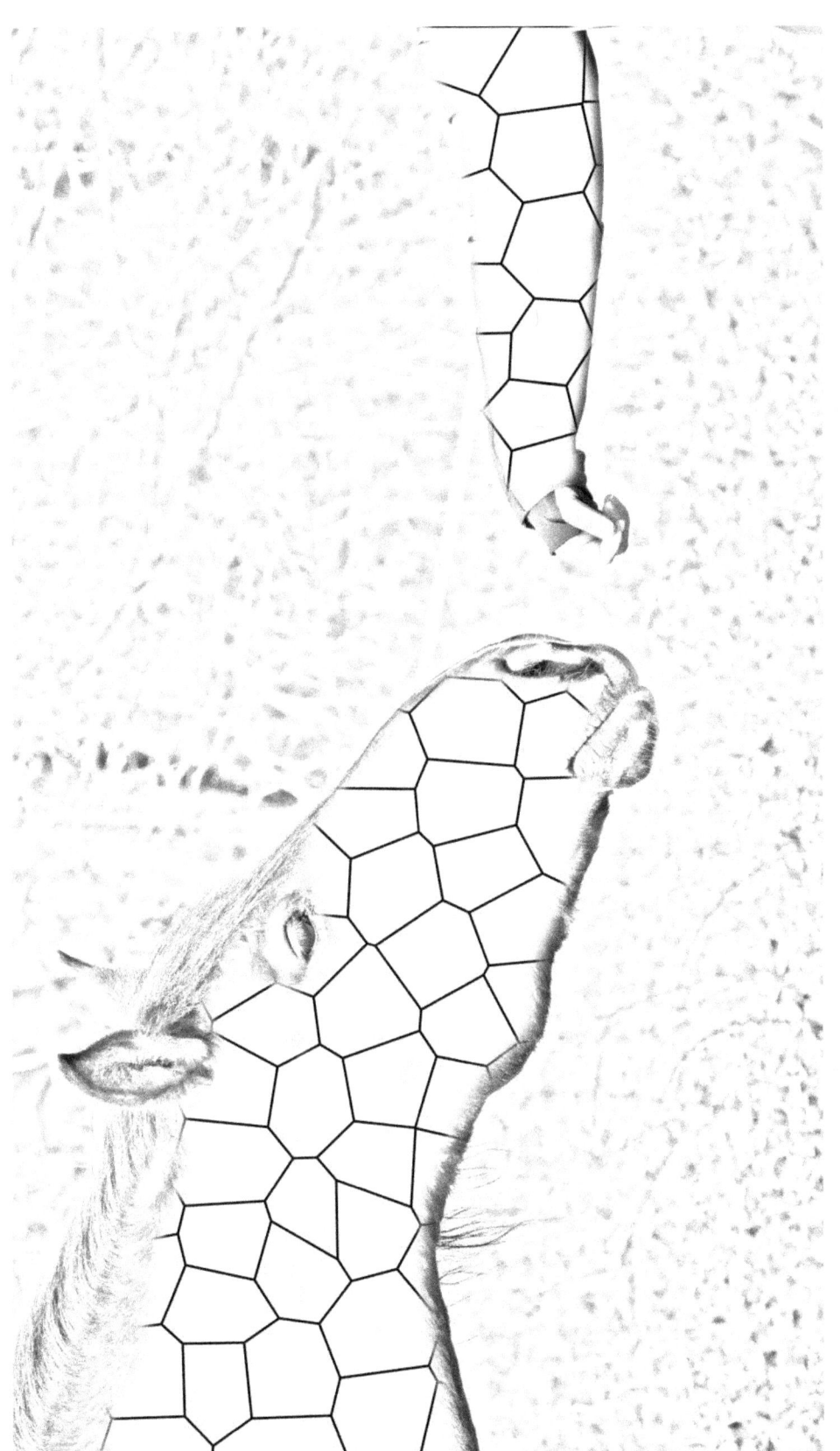

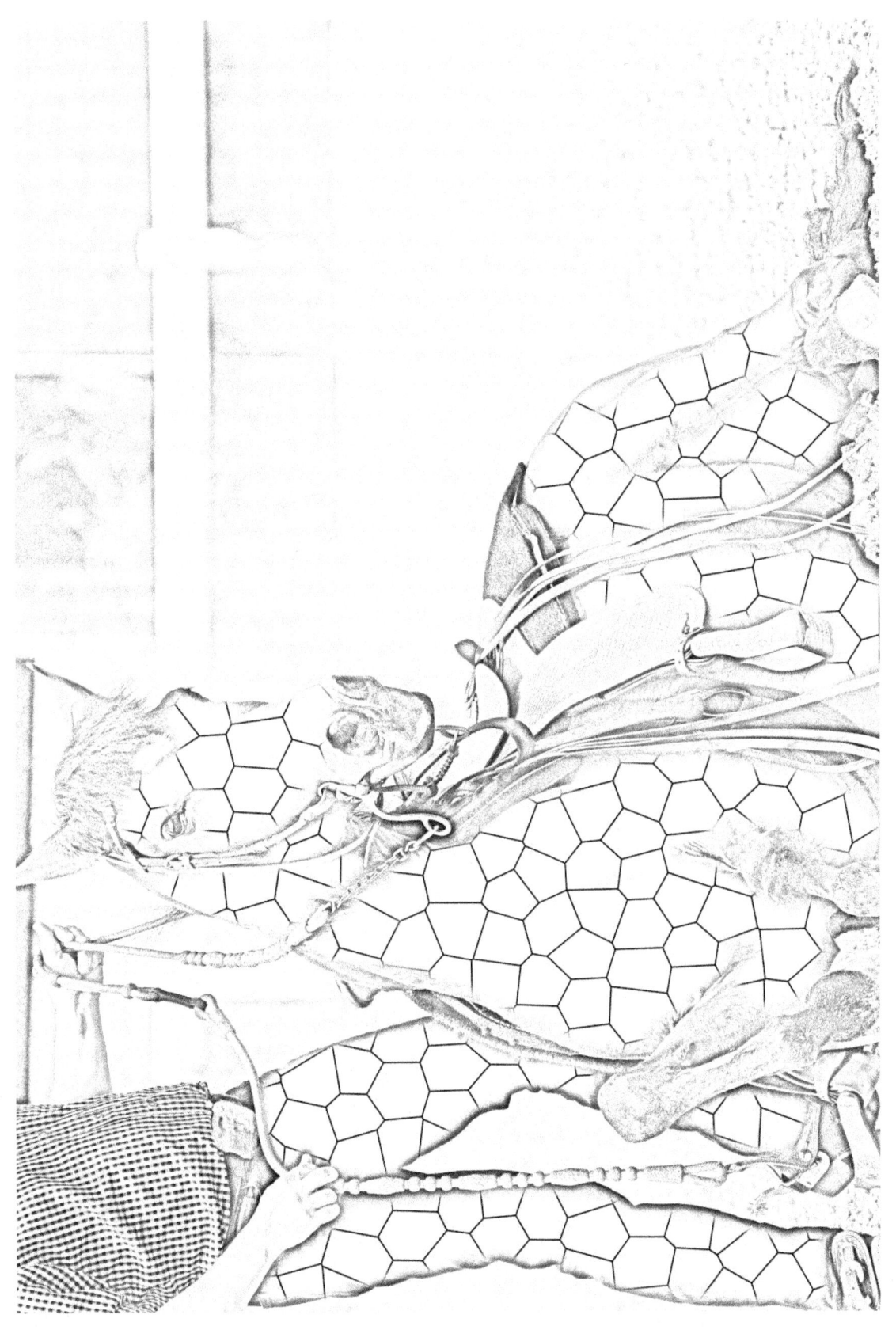

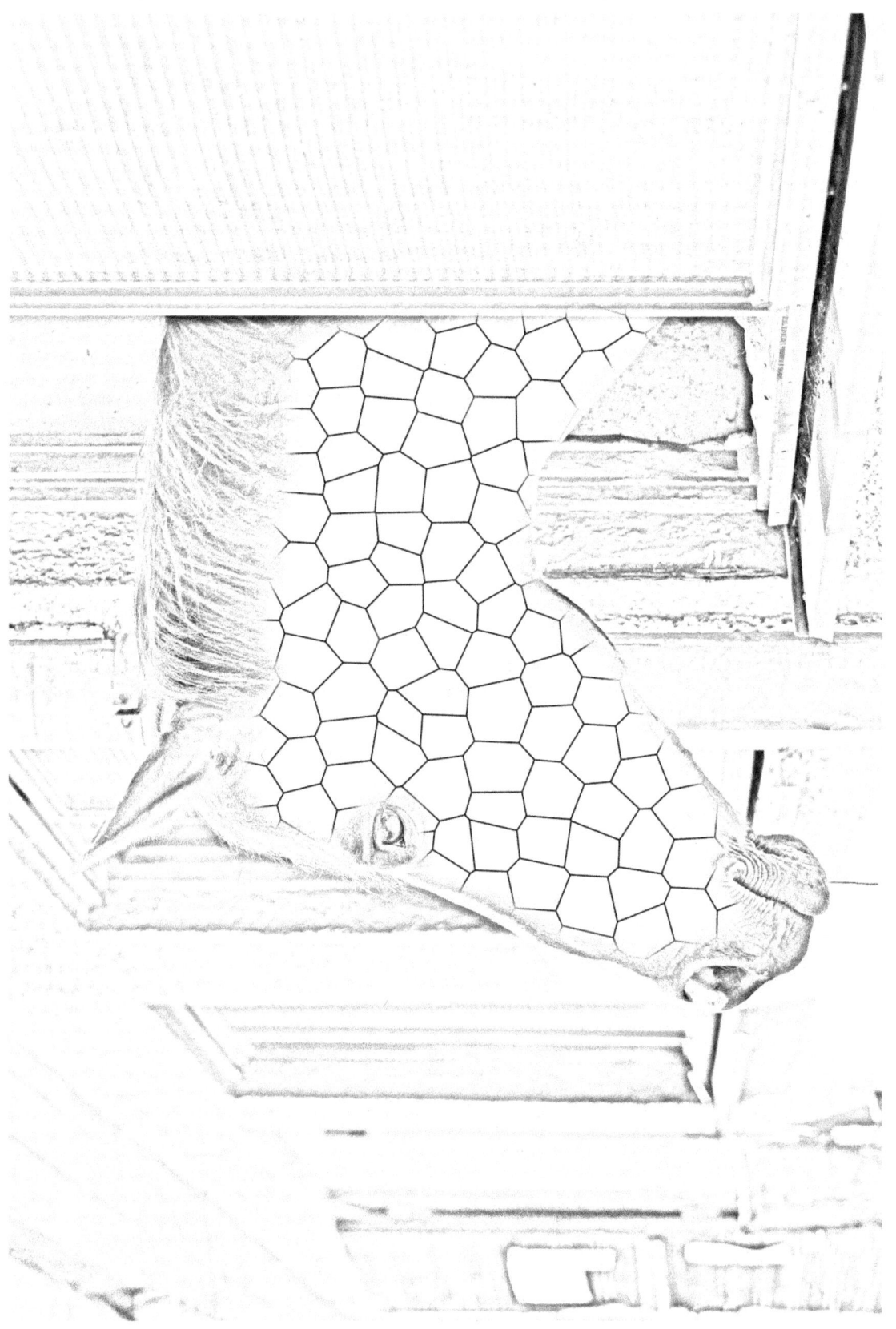

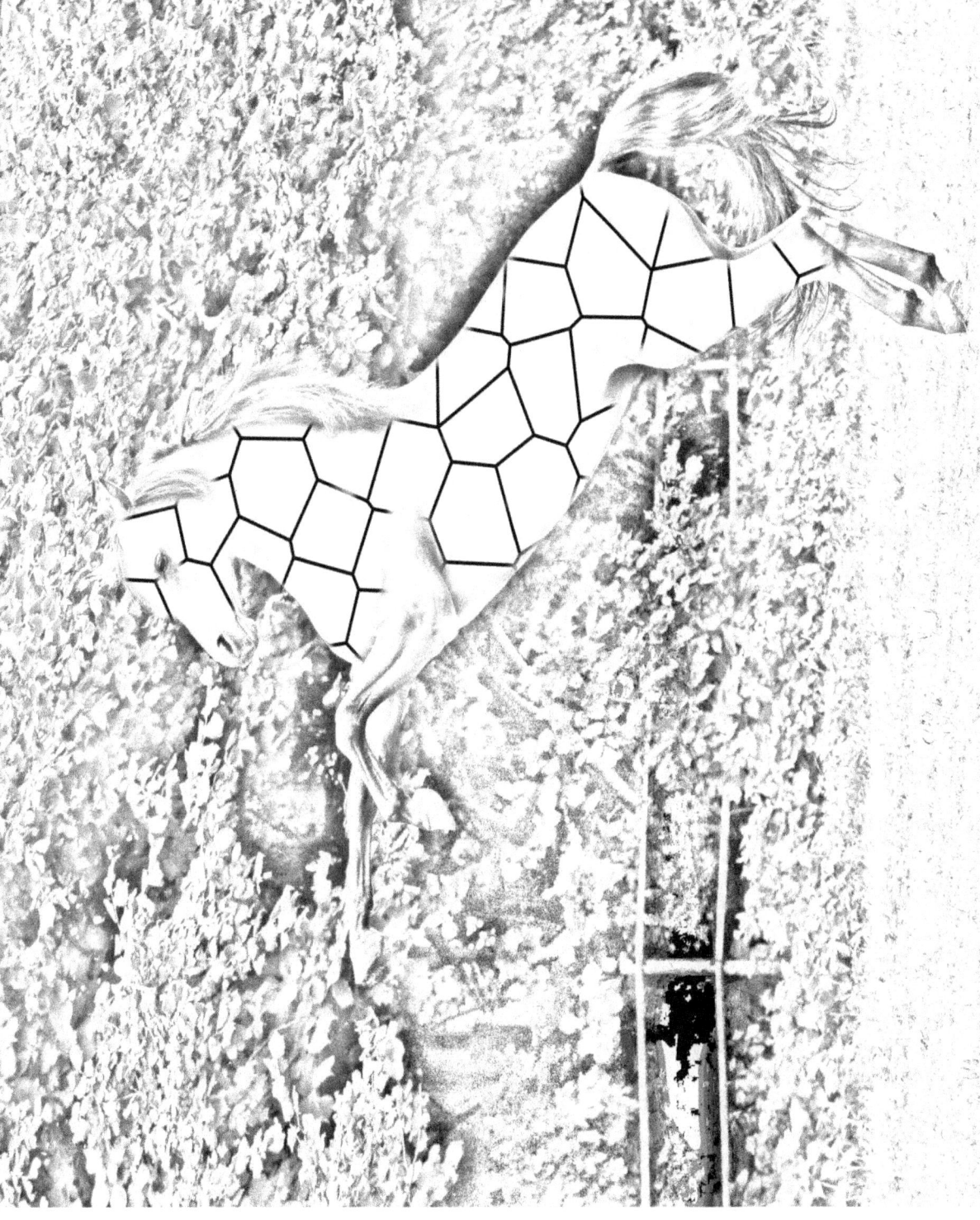

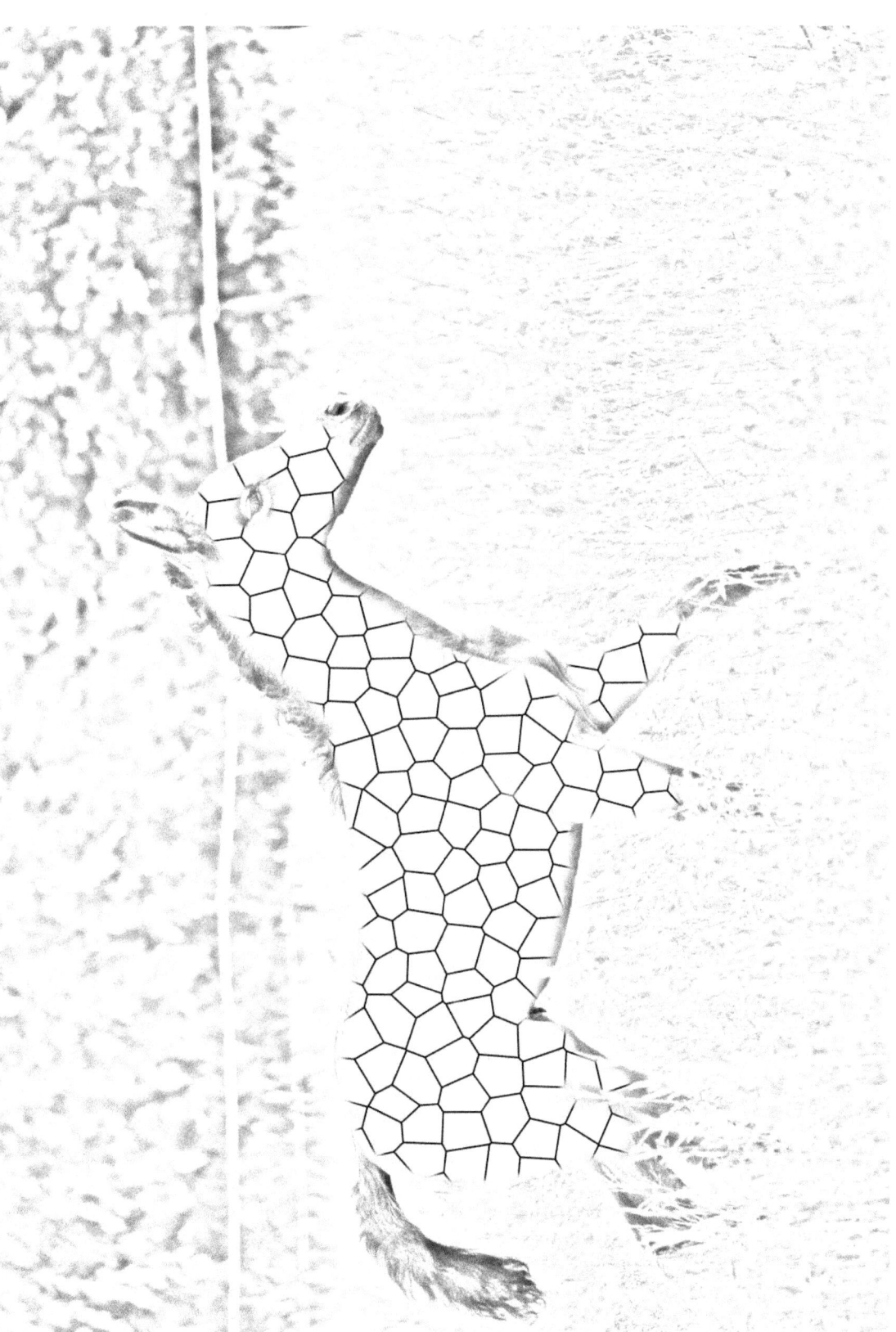

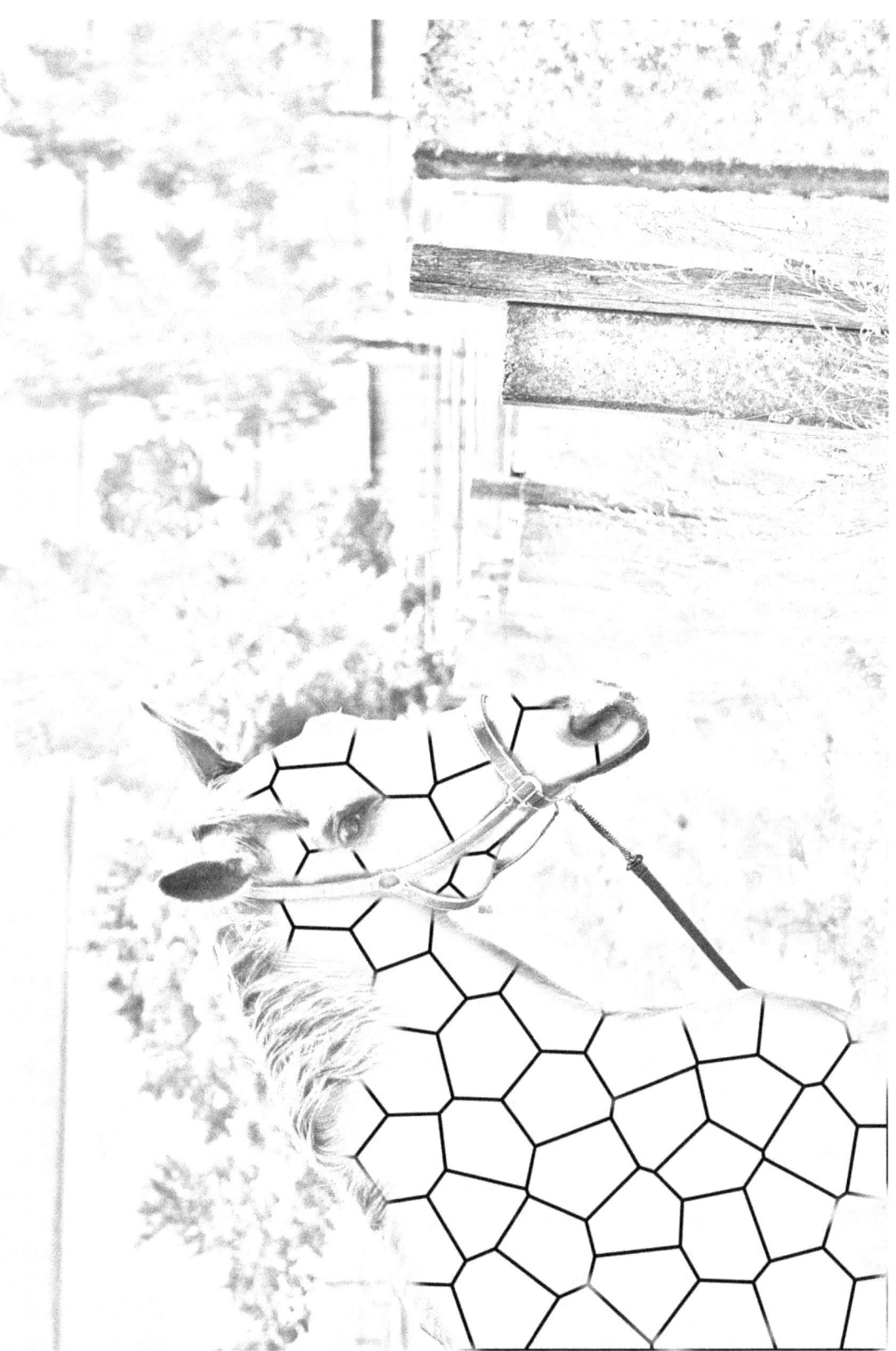

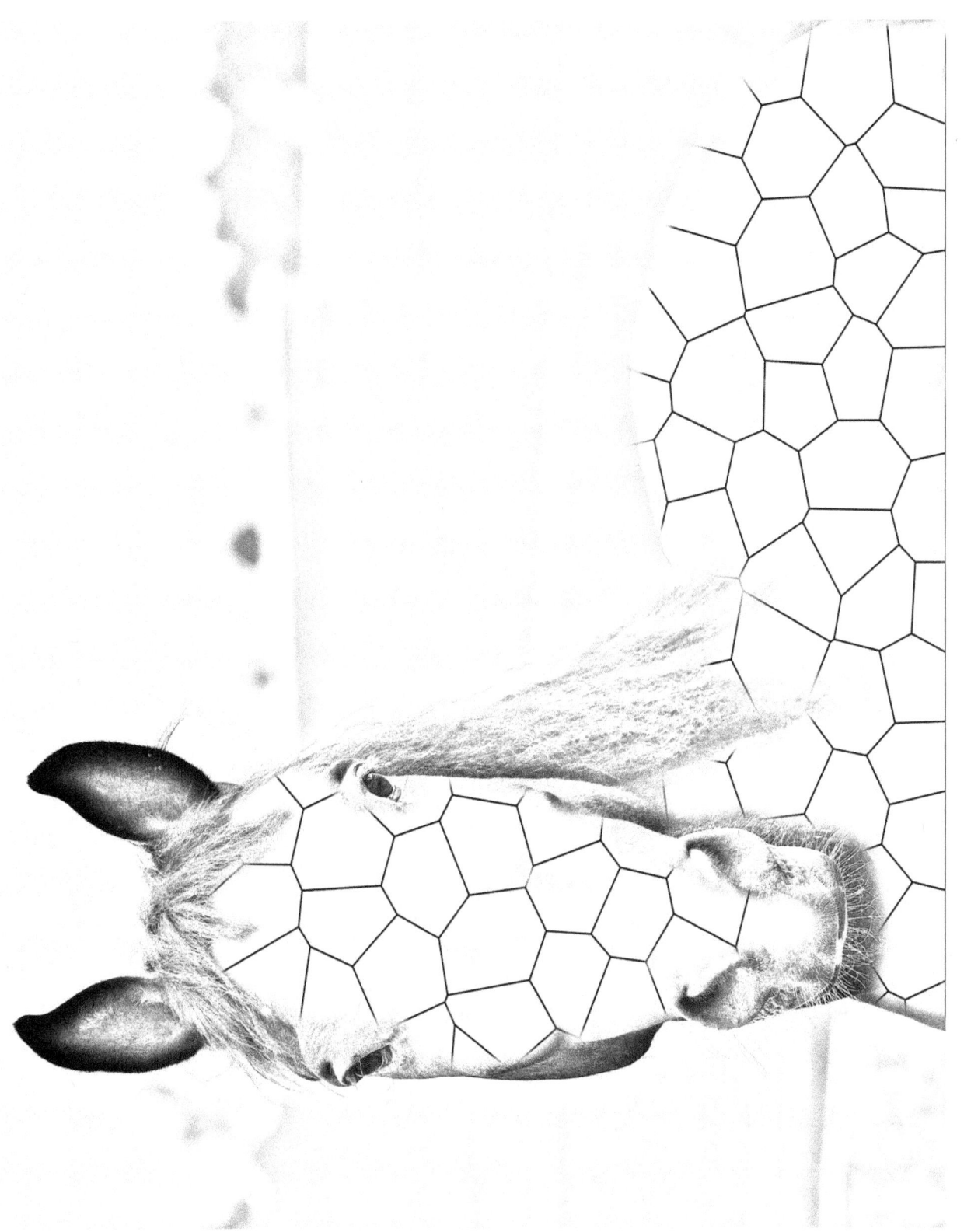

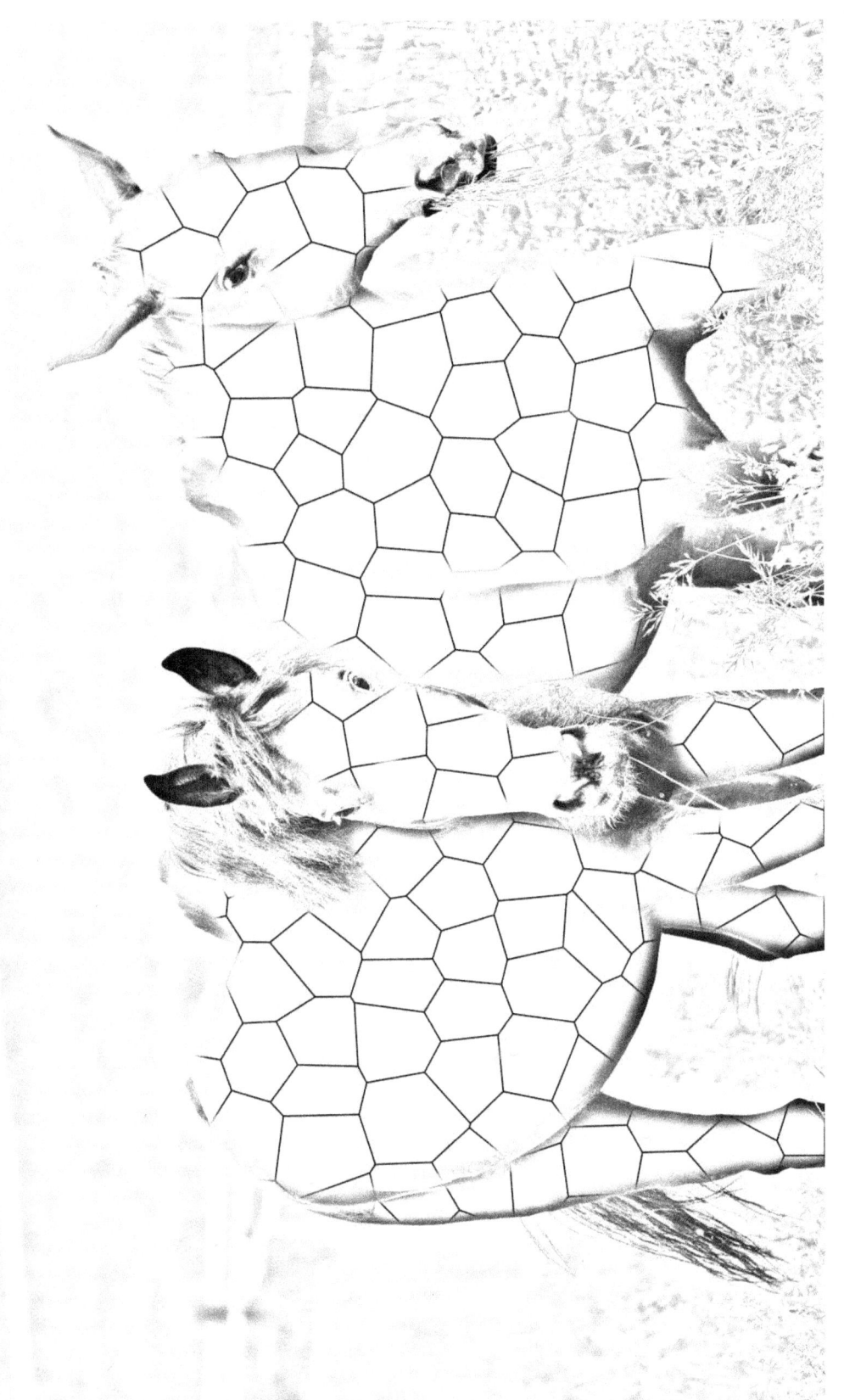

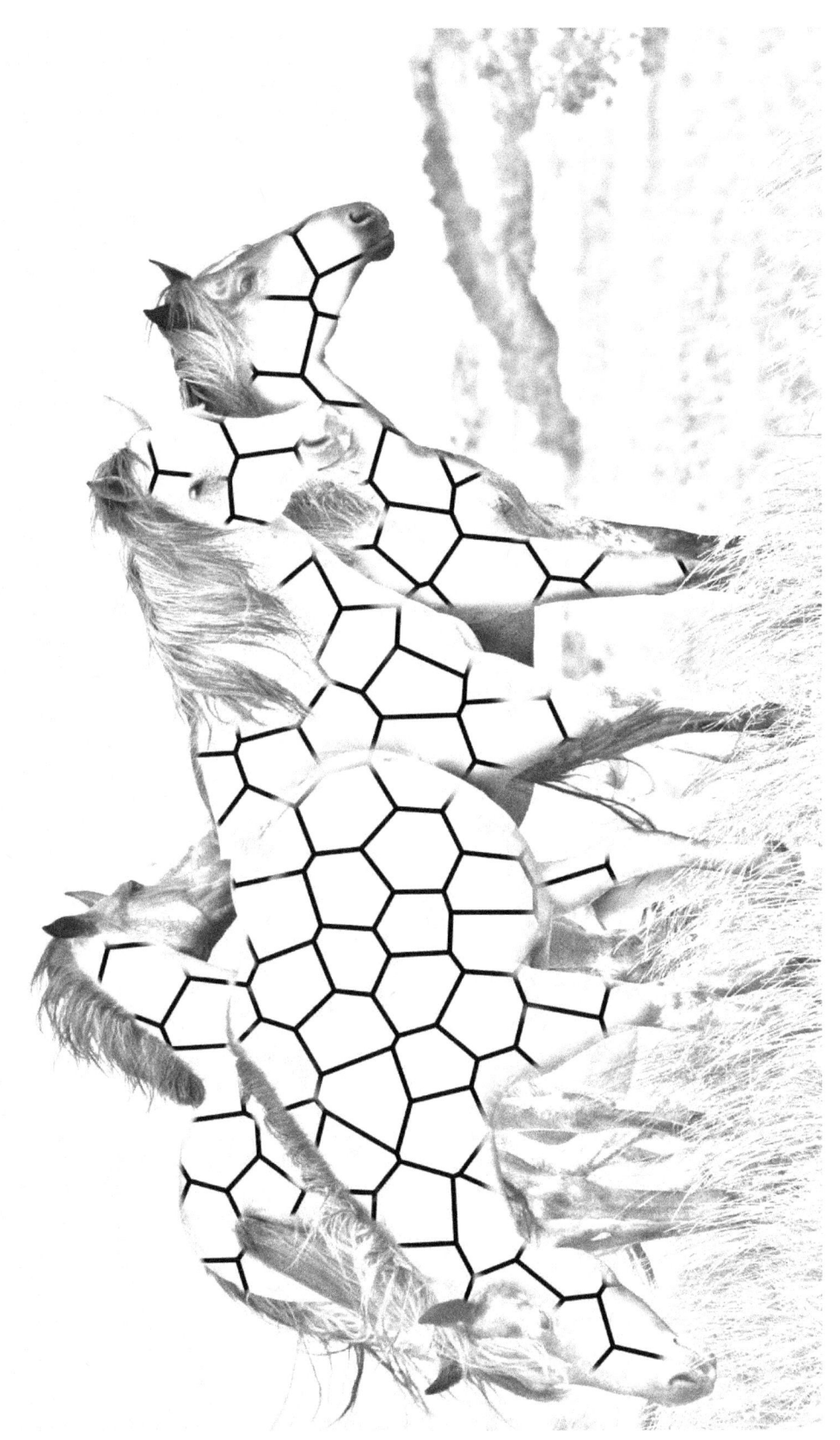

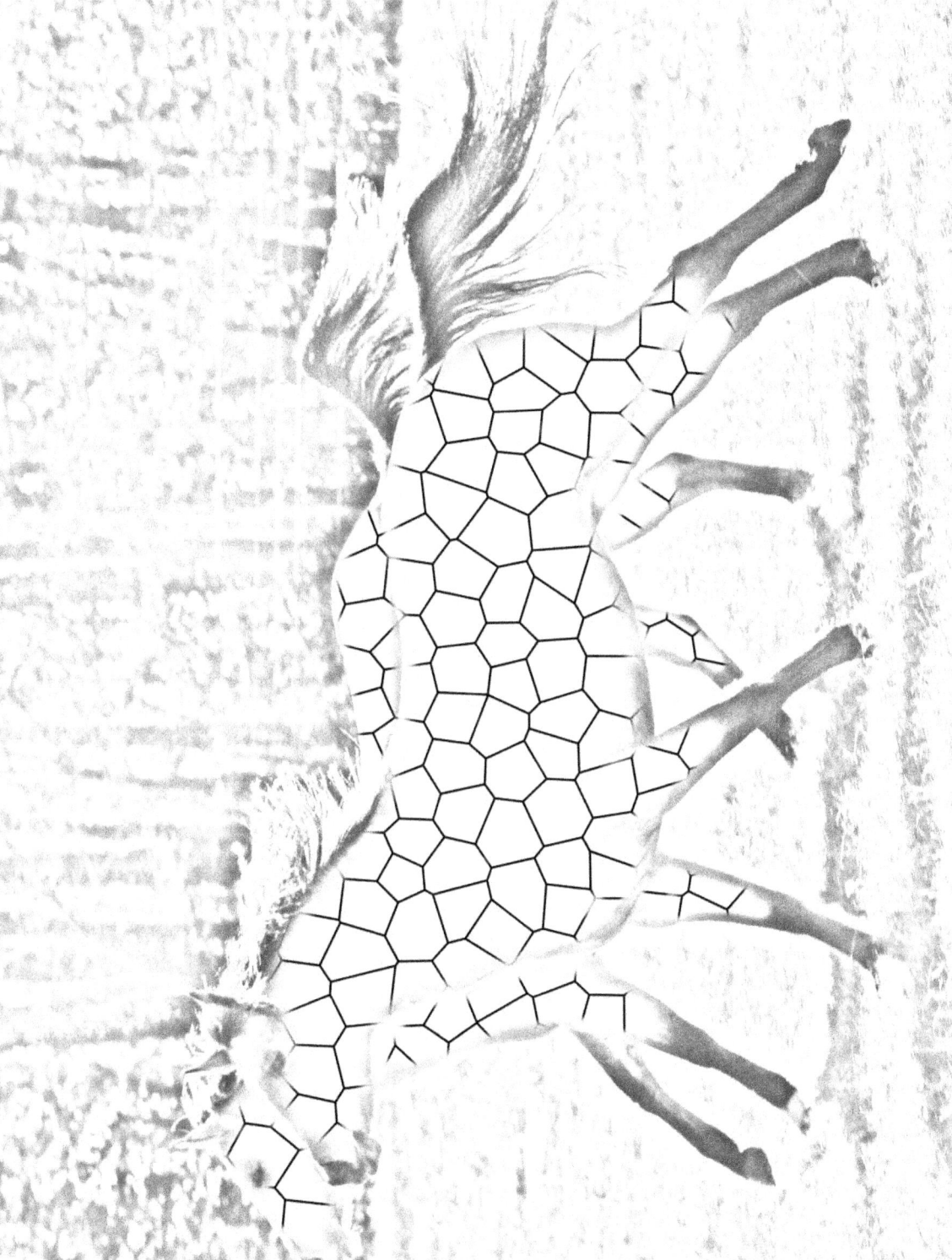

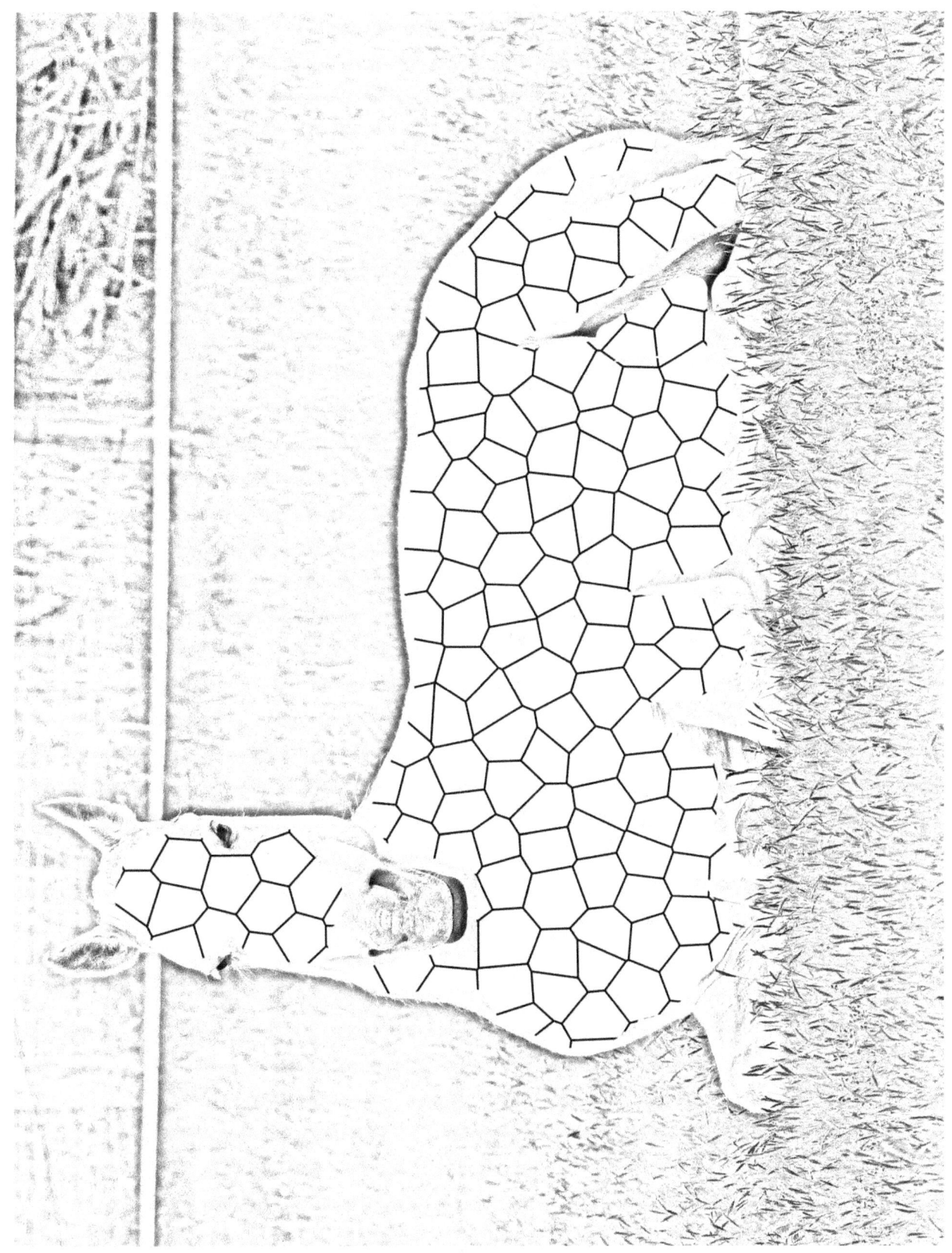

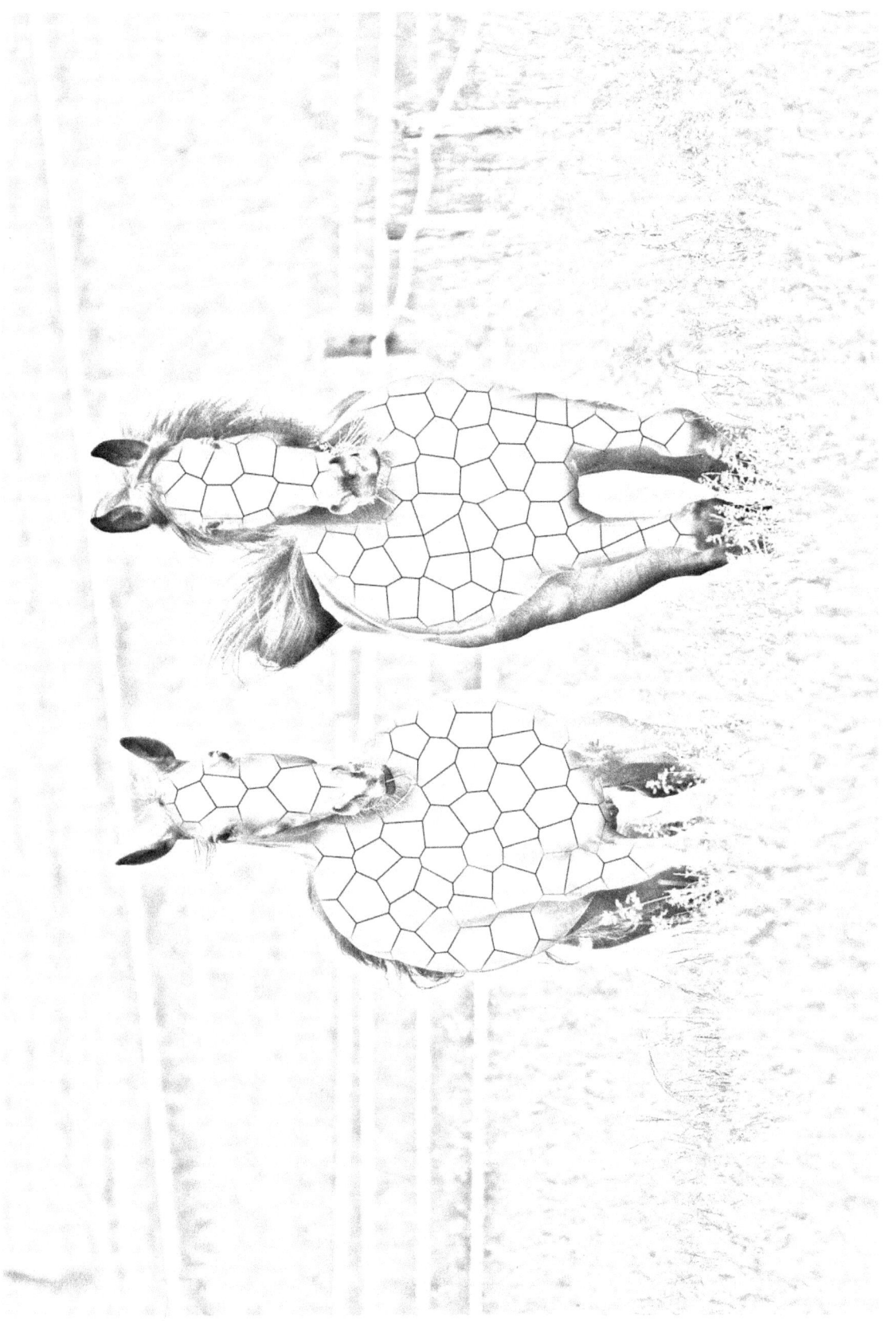

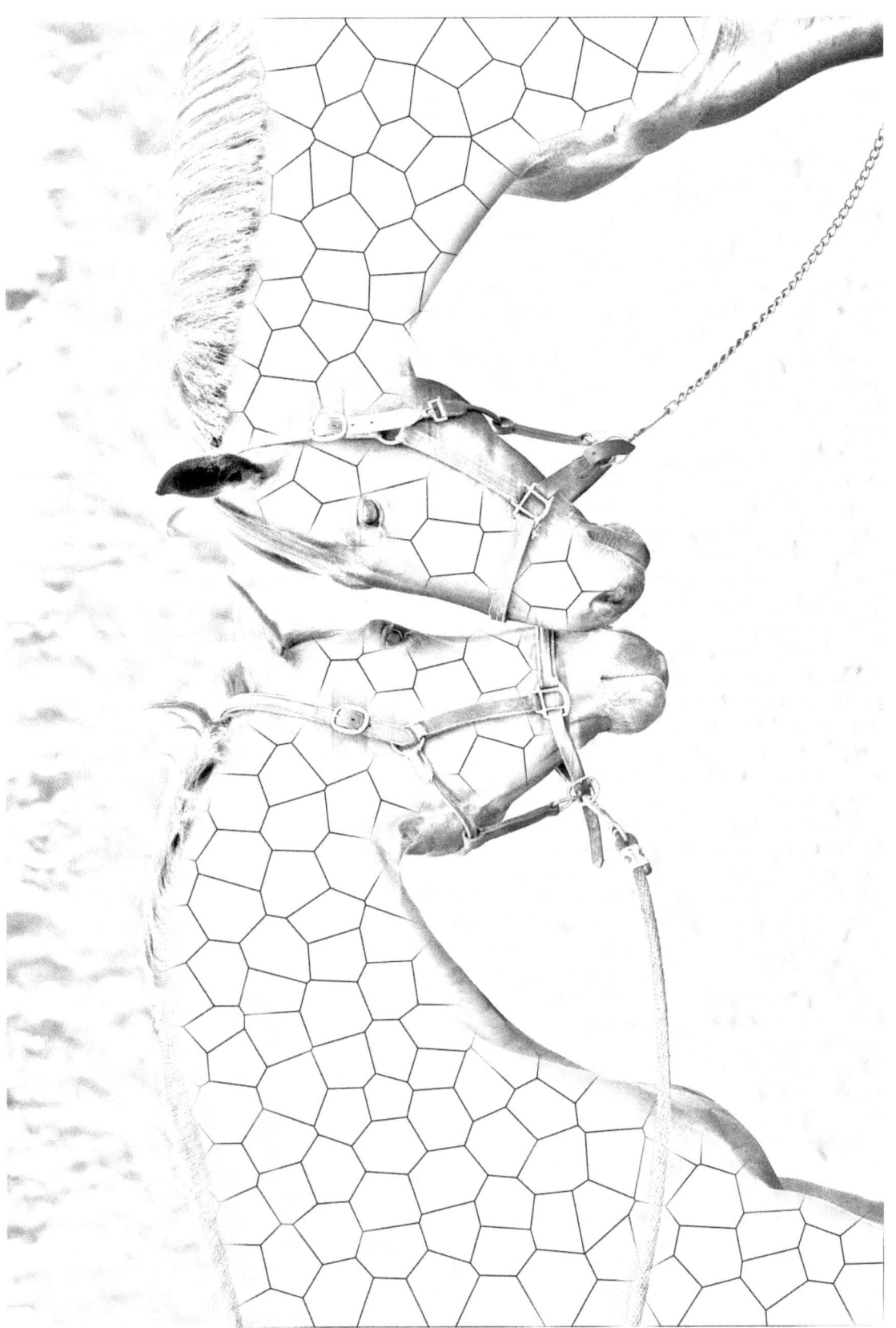

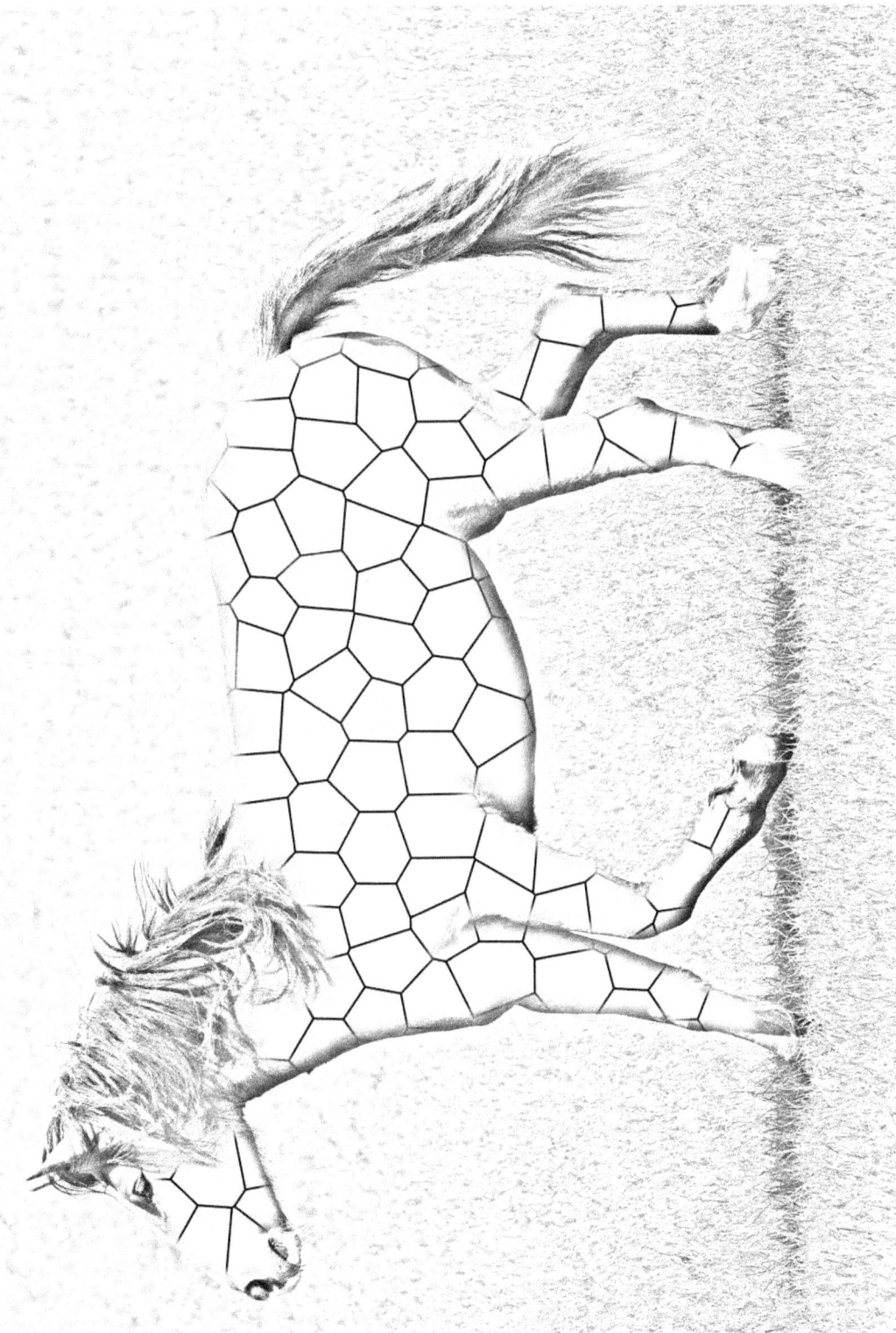

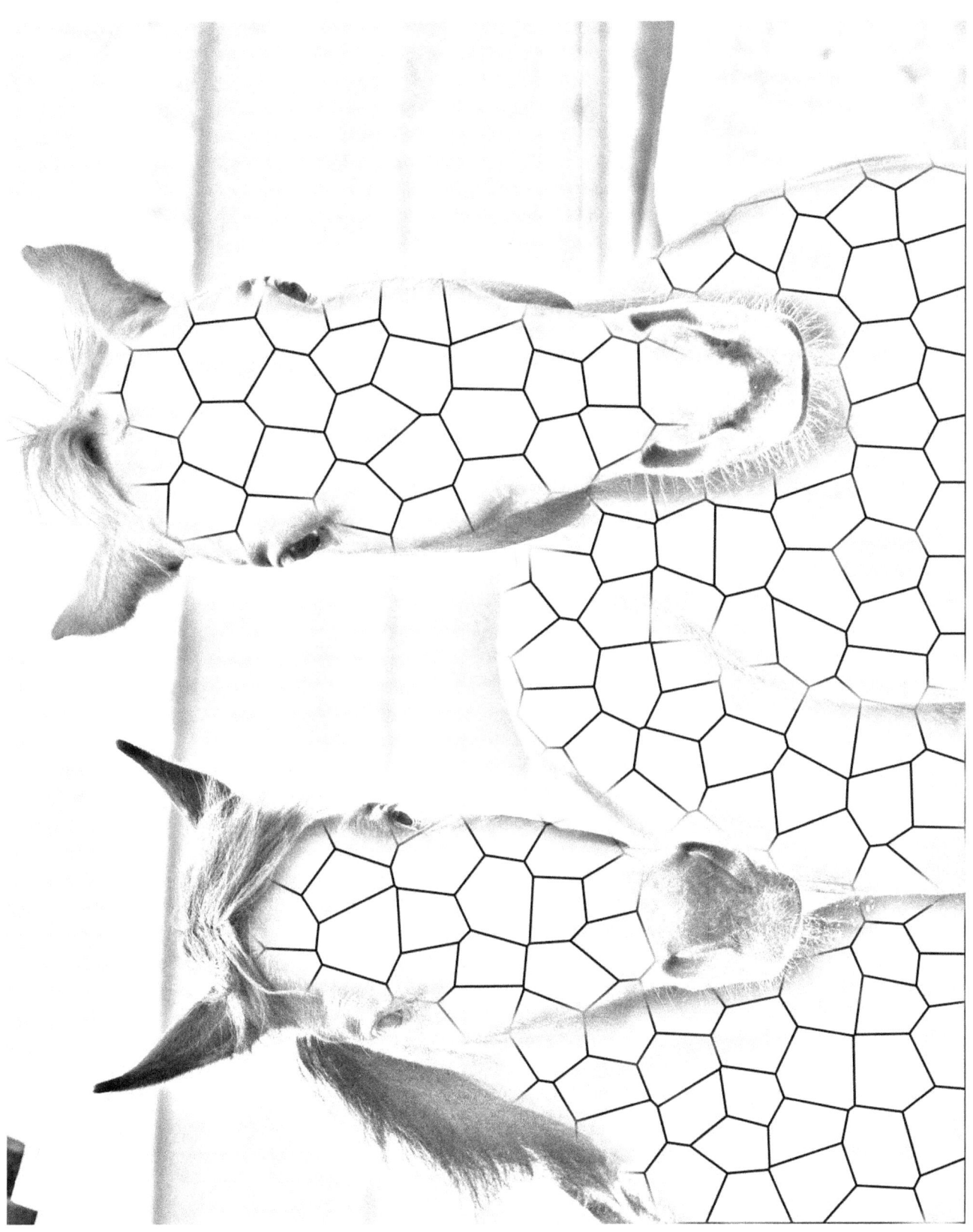

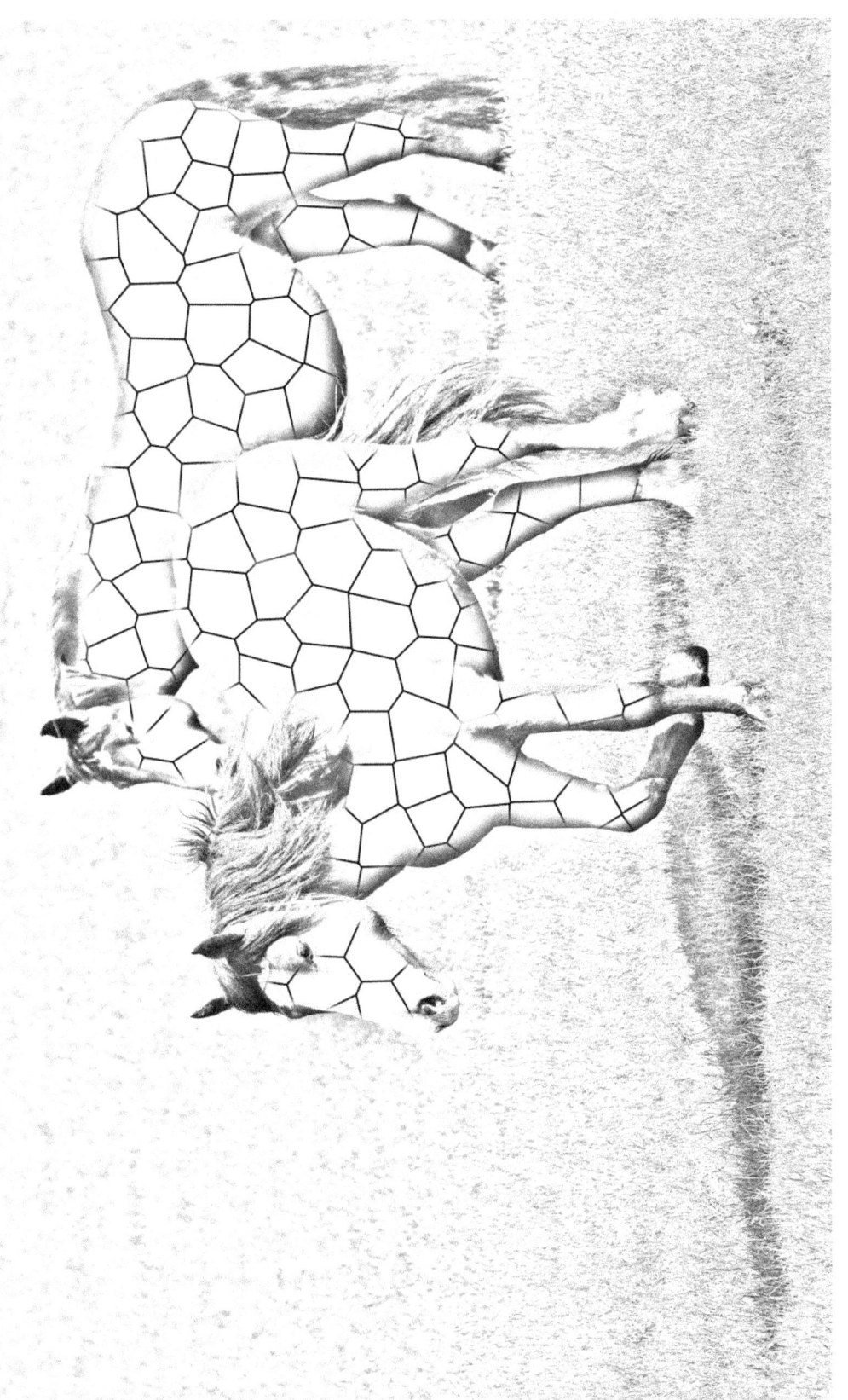

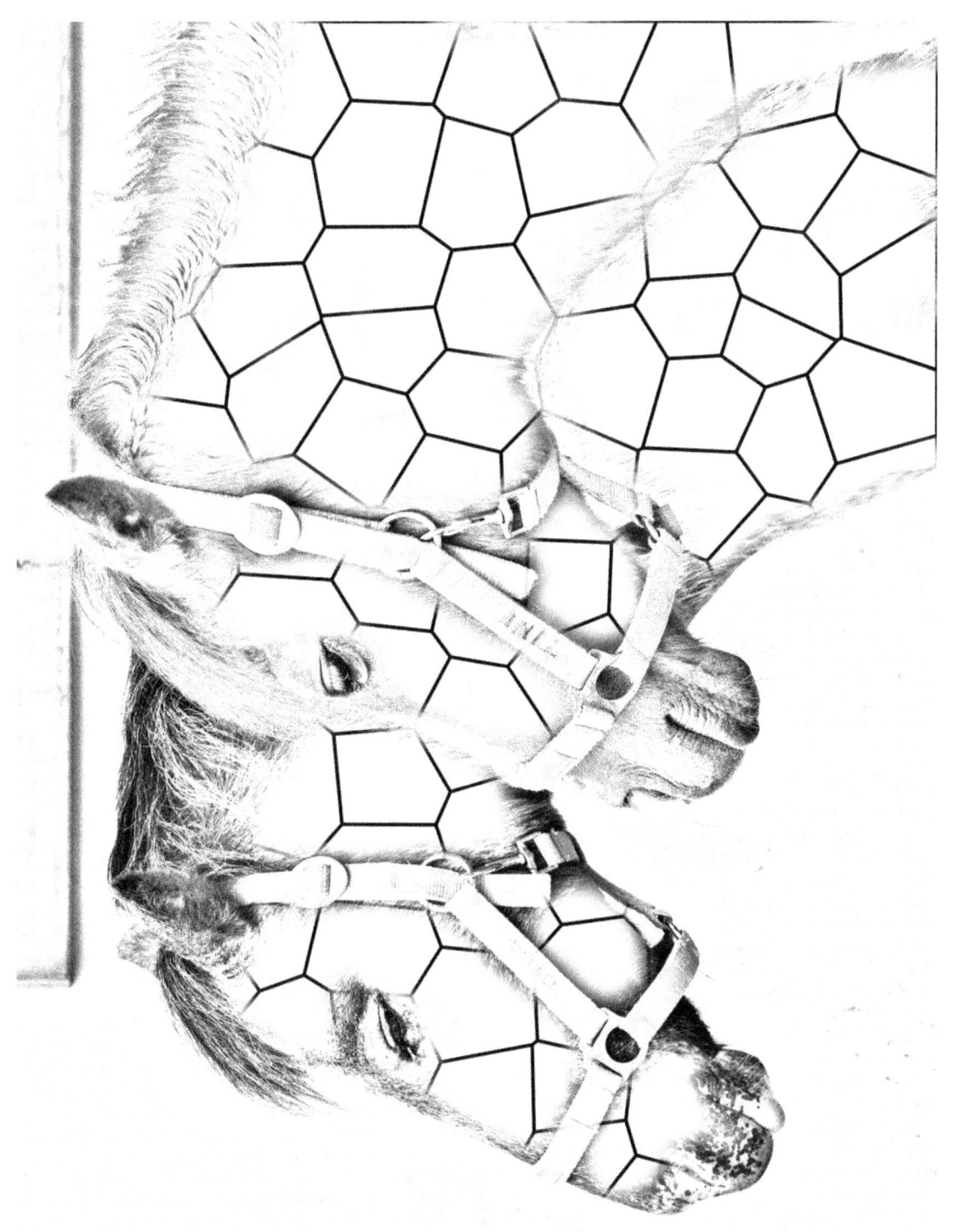

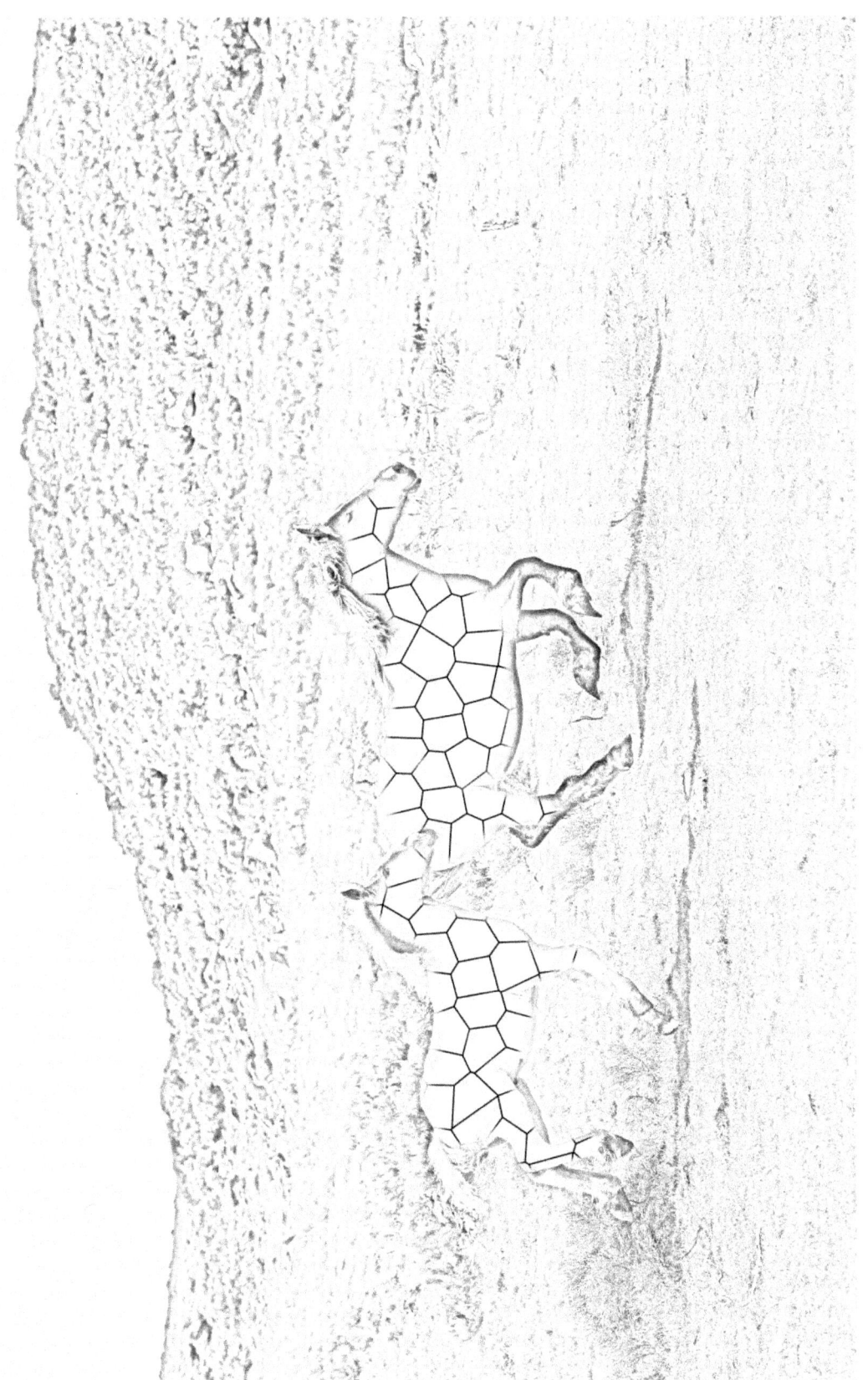

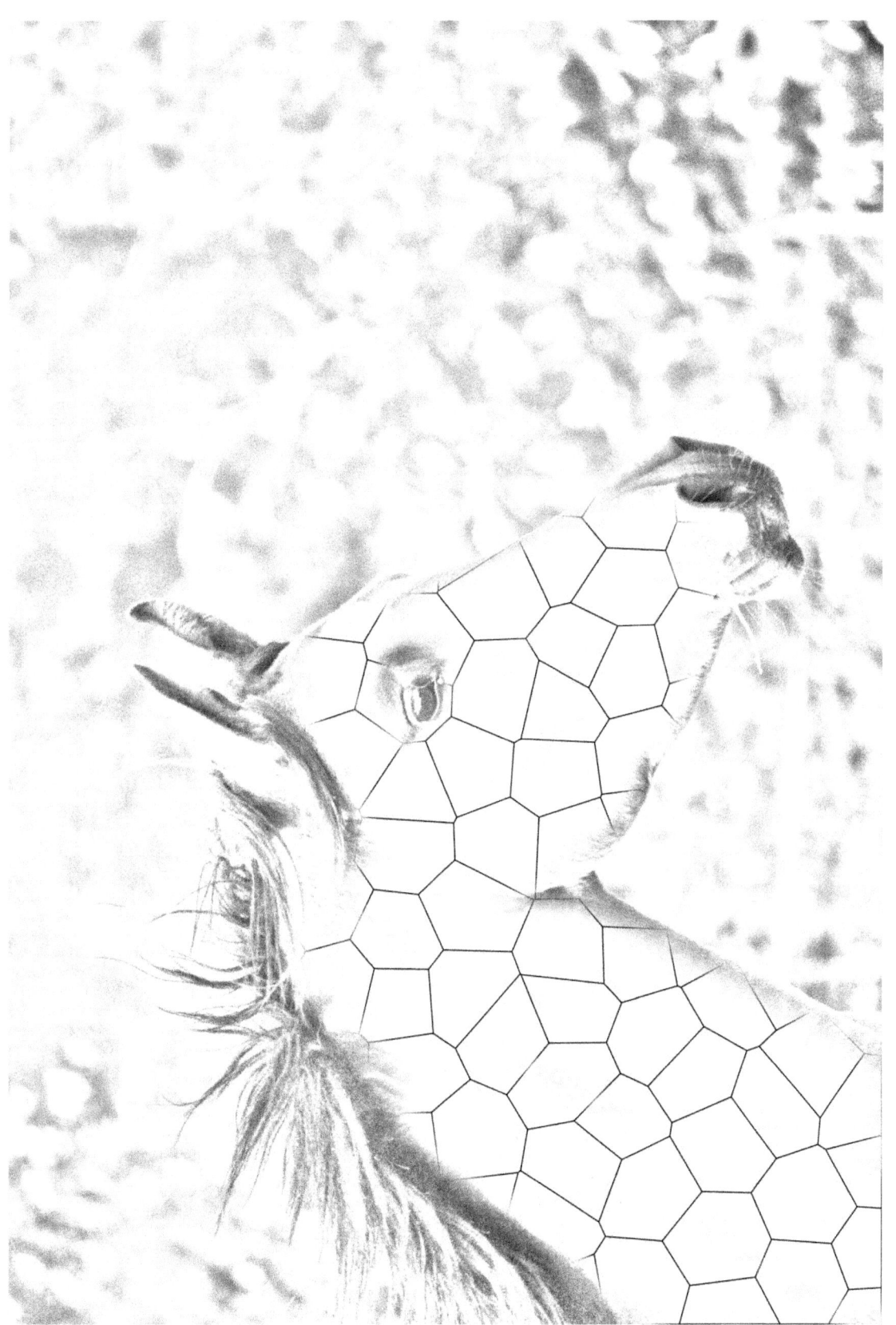

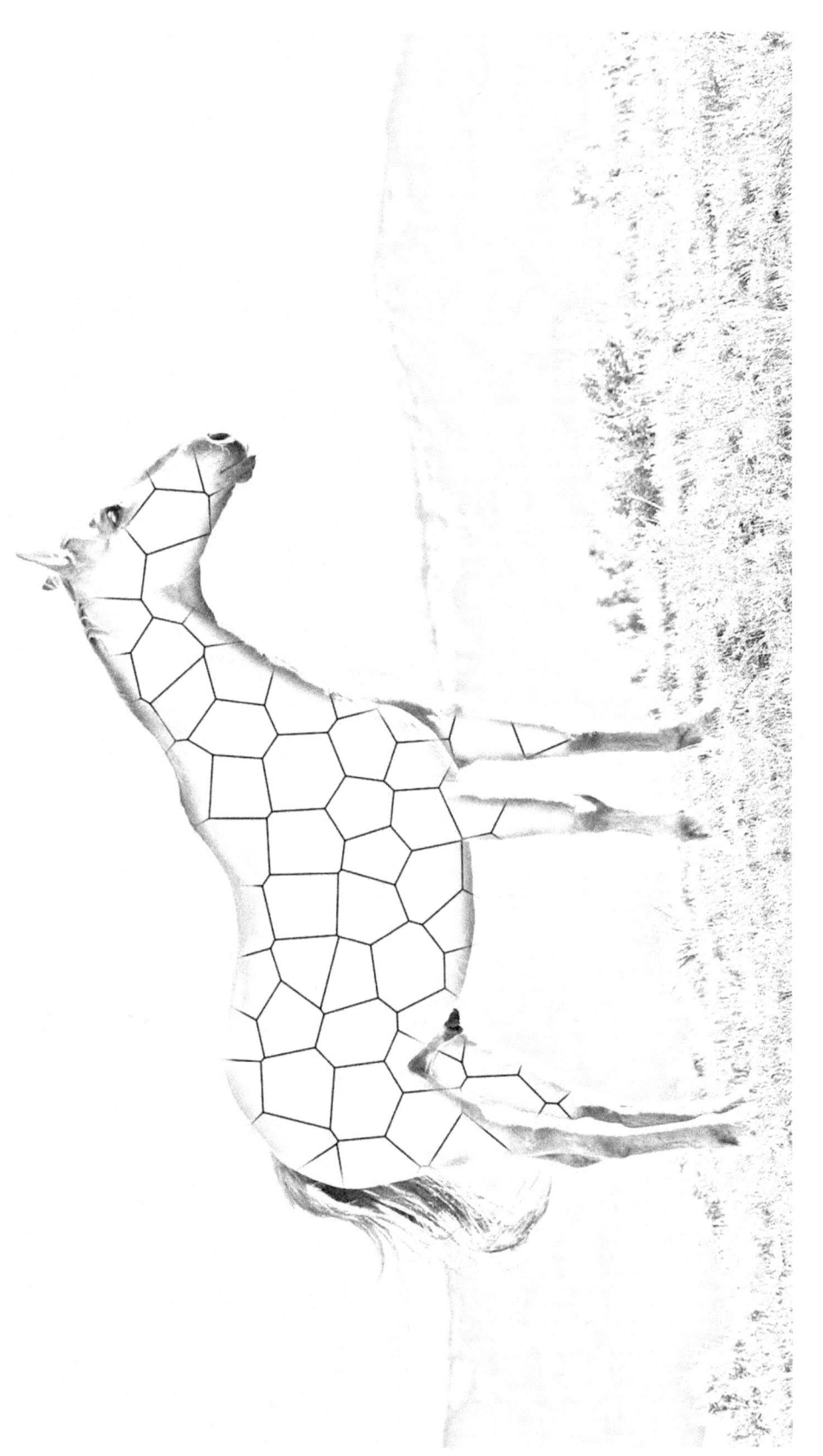

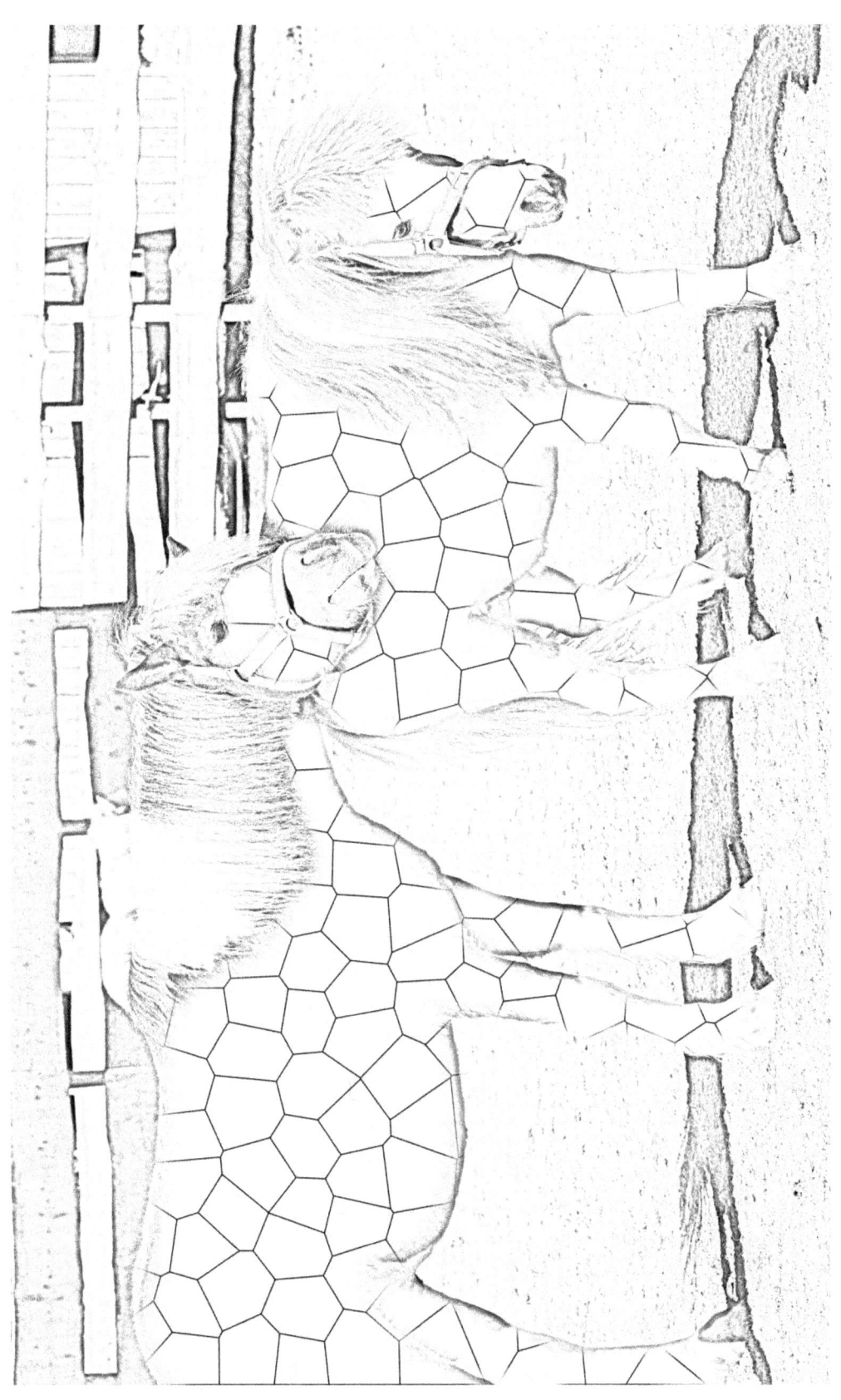

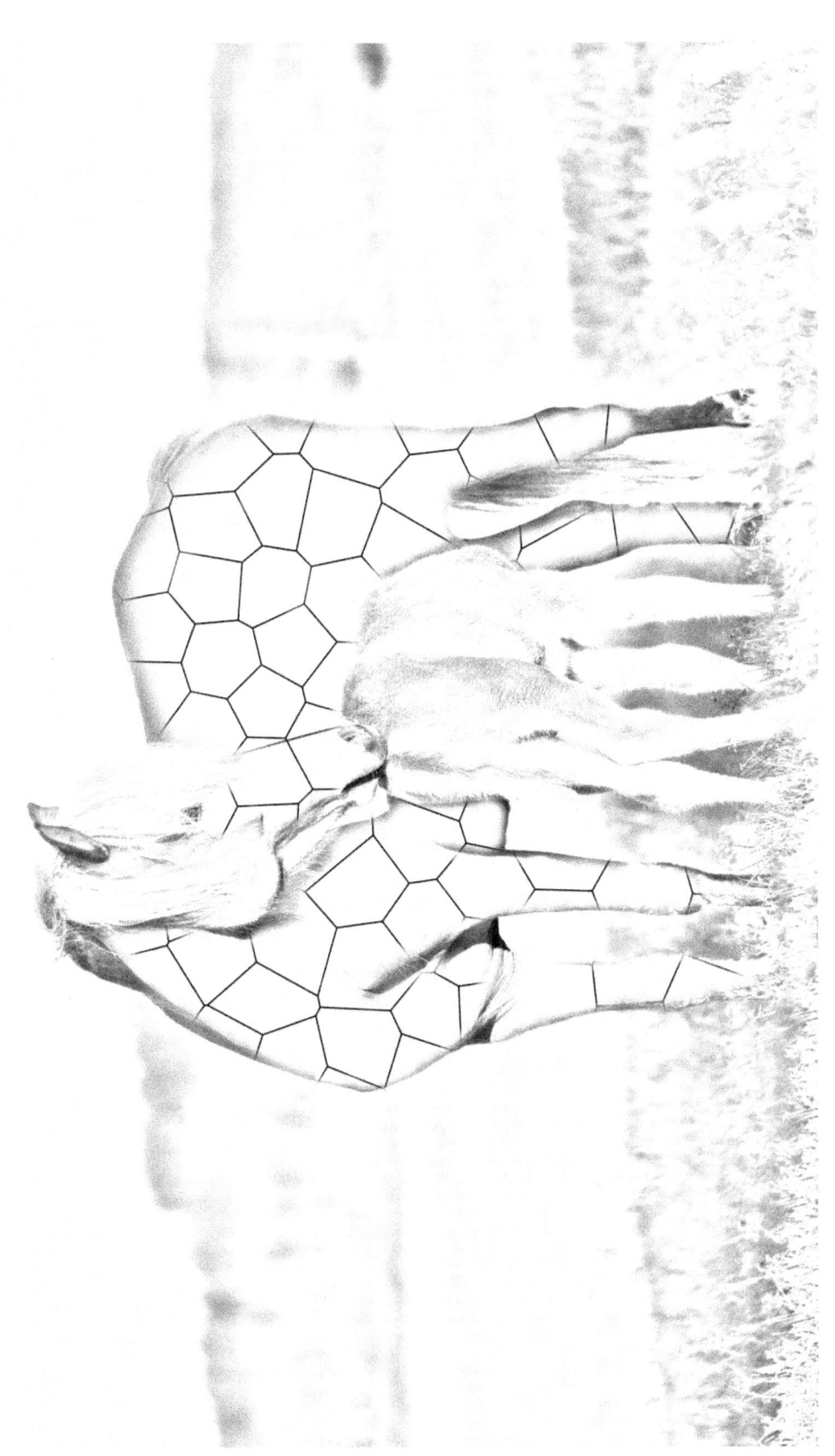